THE ANCESTRY OF MAYOR HAROLD WASHINGTON

(1922-1987)

CURTIS G. BRASFIELD

HERITAGE BOOKS, INC.

Copyright 1993 By

Curtis Brasfield

Published 1993 By

Heritage Books, Inc.
1540-E Pointer Ridge Place
Bowie, Maryland 20716
(301) 390-7709

ISBN 1-55613-750-8

A Complete Catalog Listing Hundreds Of Titles On
Genealogy, History, And Americana
Available Free On Request

DEDICATION

This genealogy is dedicated to all the Chicagoans whose lives have been touched by the late Mayor Harold Washington.

TABLE OF CONTENTS

Dedication iii

Table of Contents v

List of Genealogical Documents vii

List of Tables vii

Foreword ix

Acknowledgements xi

INTRODUCTION 1

Part I: A HISTORY OF THE WASHINGTON FAMILY 5

       Isam/Isom/Isham Washington (1832-1903) 7
          Second Marriage 9
          Genealogical Summary 11

       Isam/Isom McDaniel/Mack D. Washington (1875-1957) 14
          Move to Illinois 16
          Ministerial Career 19
          Genealogical Summary 21

       Roy Washington (1897-1953) 22
          Divorce and Remarriage 24
          Career 26
          Genealogical Summary 27

       Harold Lee Washington (1922-1987) 28
          Army Service 32
          Political Career 39
          Genealogical Summary 40

       Pedigree Chart of Harold Lee Washington 42

Part II: **METHODOLOGY USED IN RESEARCH OF THE WASHINGTON FAMILY** 45

    The Ancestry of Mayor Harold Washington 47
        Searching for Harold's father, Roy Washington:
            1900 Census 48
        Searching for Harold's grandfather, Mack Washington:
            1900 Census 50
        Searching for Harold's great-grandfather, Isam
            Washington: 1900 Census 51
        Moving Forward: the 1910 Census 52
        Collateral Lines: the 1880 Census 53

    Researching Records 54
        Probate Records 55
        Ballard County Land and Tax Records 55
        Military Records of Isham Washington 59
        Pension Records of Isham and Elizabeth
            Washington 60
        Elizabeth (Howell) Washington 72
        Isam's Children:
            Sallie Washington 72
            William P. Washington 72
        Learning More about Isam Washington in the 1870s
            and 1880s 74
        The Origin of Isam Washington's Surname 74
        Massac County Vital Records: Arbella (Hamilton)
            Weeks's Genealogy 76

CONCLUSION 83

Appendix A: A Brief History of Ballard County 83

Appendix B: Civilian Conservation Corps Records of Harold Washington 87

Appendix C: Military Service Records of Harold Washington 95

Appendix D: Harold Washington's Ancestry Place Sorted List 101

Glossary 107

Bibliography 109

Index 111

LIST OF GENEALOGICAL DOCUMENTS

Figure 1.	County map for the state of Kentucky.	15
Figure 2.	St. James A.M.E. Church, 1988.	18
Figure 3.	Marriage license of Roy Washington and Bertha Jones.	23
Figure 4.	Photograph of Roy Washington and classmates.	25
Figure 5.	St. Benedict's School record of Harold L. Washington.	29
Figure 6.	Marriage license of Harold Washington and Nancy Dorothy Finch.	31
Figure 7.	Photograph of Pvt. Harold Washington (1943).	33
Figure 8.	Photograph of Sgt. Harold Washington (1945).	37
Figure 9.	DuSable High School graduating roster (1946).	38
Figure 10.	Photograph of Harold Washington monument (1991).	41
Figure 11.	Pedigree chart of Harold Washington.	43
Figure 12.	Death certificate of Roy L. Washington.	49
Figure 13.	Civil War military records of Isham Washington.	66
Figure 14.	Marriage license of Isam Washington and Mary Elizabeth (Howell) Frasier.	67
Figure 15.	Isam Washington dropped from pension roster.	69
Figure 16.	Mary Elizabeth Washington dropped from pension roster.	70
Figure 17.	Isam Washington's pension application.	71
Figure 18.	Decatur, Illinois city directory.	75
Figure 19.	Marriage register of Mack Washington and Arbella Weeks.	77

LIST OF TABLES

Table 1.	Tax records of Isam/Isham Washington.	57
Table 2.	Mortgage records of Isam/Isham Washington.	61
Table 3.	Mortgage record of J.A. Washington.	64
Table 4.	Mortgage records of W.P. Washington.	65

FOREWORD

This ancestry was researched, compiled and presented here for anyone who is interested in learning more about the late Harold Washington's ancestors and family roots. The compiled genealogy shows the known ancestors of Harold Washington, who was elected and served as Chicago's first African-American mayor from 1983 until his death in November, 1987. As mayor of the third largest city in America, he symbolized hope for many Chicagoans as well as many minorities and ethnic groups at the grassroots level nationwide. Articles and books have been written about his life as a politician, yet little is known or has been written about his family life. Bits and pieces of information about his early childhood and family life have been found scattered in many newspapers, magazines and books. The author has carefully researched and assembled these pieces with documented sources and presented them in this book so that the reader can get a clearer picture of the life and times of the late mayor.

Much of the information is presented here for the first time. For example, no other book or article has mentioned that Harold Washington's great-grandfather was a slave and served in the Civil War. This book has been designed with the reader and researcher in mind. It not only names the known ancestors of Harold Washington but provides the methods and sources used by genealogists to research ancestry. Maps and illustrations drawn from actual documents are used to support the narrative text of the author. The material for this book is the result of six years of collecting and compiling primary and secondary records by the author, who is a Certified Genealogical Record Searcher (C.G.R.S.). It is accurate as far as known, but additional information and corrections probably can be found. Research should be continued in an attempt to locate any records that will shed additional light on Harold Washington's family lineage.

ACKNOWLEDGEMENTS

Thanks to:

Thaddeus Jackson, who initiated the Washington Family genealogy research project in 1984 and presented his findings in an oral report at an African-American Genealogy Workshop in February, 1985, at the Cultural Center with the late Mayor Washington's permission.

Mrs. Roberta L. Senor of Springfield, Illinois, who was a personal friend of the Washington family, as well as a member of St. John A.M.E. Church where Rev. I.M.D. Washington served as pastor. She sent invaluable information regarding the late Mayor Washington's grandparents.

Mr. and Mrs. Carl R. Curry of Bridgeport, Illinois, who are members of the Lawrence County Genealogical Society and members of the present St. James A.M.E. Church of Lawrenceville, Illinois, where Rev. I.M.D. Washington was founder and pastor, for sending me pictures and newspaper articles documenting Rev. Washington's church records dating back to 1915.

A special thanks goes to Kathryn R. Nielson (Utah), Kathie Mauzey (California), and Martha S. Stamper and Iris Winkler (Kentucky) for their help and advice.

INTRODUCTION

The search for historical records linking the different generations of Black Americans is known to most of us as African-American genealogy. Every February millions of people observe Black History Month. They learn many dates, names, and inventions and "firsts" accomplished by Black Americans. These accomplishments make us proud of our forefathers and our heritage, and help everybody — including other ethnic groups — to know the *real* contributions by African-Americans. By keeping the study of Black history alive, we can continue to rescue our history from racist distortions and omissions.

When we study genealogy and our own family lines, we can go much deeper into our history. We get a clearer picture of how a particular family lived and survived. We discover achievements — often against great odds — and the problems which have affected different generations in different periods of history. We can use our families, therefore, as a basis for understanding how other African-Americans have lived, suffered, struggled, and made changes so that others of us would have better lives. This knowledge puts us in the center of Black history as a continuing movement of struggle. We are no longer merely interested observers looking at our pasts — we are committed. For just as previous generations helped to shape the world we live in now, we must in turn be the generation that changes and shapes tomorrow into a world based on freedom and democracy for *all* people.

African-American Genealogy. Genealogy in America did not begin until around the late 1700s. Although the study of ancestors dates back to biblical times, its progress in this country was slow in the beginning, and it did not actually develop on a large scale for White genealogists until the 1800s. Family origin was almost totally neglected by generations of Black people with African roots.

With the publication of Alex Haley's *Roots*, Black historians and genealogists became inspired to dig deeper into their African ancestry. The great surge of interest in the subject was due not only to Haley's award-winning book but probably more to the award-winning TV dramatization of the book. The amazing saga of one family's journey through history refreshed the memories of older Blacks living in America and acquainted younger generations with a sad but true chapter in African-American history.

Before *Roots* was aired on national television, genealogy was considered by many to be for the wealthy upper class. (Fortunately, Alex

Haley had the financial backing of his publisher and the movie industry.) Now, genealogy is for anyone who wants to know who he is and who his ancestors were. *Roots* was important because it demonstrated that genealogy knows no color, age, class, or national origin, but is open to anyone who has the desire to search for his history. The TV dramatization of *Roots* was particularly inspiring for Black Americans.

The growing interest in genealogy has prompted many families, schools, community groups, and special clubs and organizations to develop research projects in an effort to preserve their heritages. Many educators are discovering that as students learn to understand records that were kept in the distant past, and the forces that influenced a family, they will become more familiar with geography, history, government, religion, and economics.

Research Challenge. Patience and persistence are the greatest attributes for one who decides to trace his ancestry. African-American genealogy, a new field, is considered a difficult task by genealogists and historians because of the lack of written records before and during slavery. Genealogical research on Blacks presents challenges well beyond those customarily encountered in studies of White families. Blacks who pursue the challenge discover early in their research that records for Blacks are relatively scarce and inadequate for genealogical research purposes. The source materials needed are quite different from those for Whites, since the majority of the "how-to" books were written by Whites for Whites.

The source materials compiled in major genealogical societies rarely contain any information pertaining to Blacks, and seldom, if ever, use the words *colored, Negro, Afro-American,* or *African-American.* This is not surprising when you realize that Black people were brought to America forcibly during the 17th, 18th, and 19th centuries in order to supply the labor force needed to build this country. There are few written records for individual families, since Black families were bought, sold, auctioned, and shifted about much like livestock. Often, families were split up, either on the auction block or by their owners after purchase.

Opposition to slavery arose quickly. African-Americans fought it overtly and covertly through such methods as suicide, individual or mass infanticide, hunger strikes, destroying of property, poisoning of owners, feigning illness, self-injury to avoid working, setting fire to fields and houses, running away, plotting with Indians against settlers, and joining the British forces during the Revolutionary War. Escapes were legion. But not all Black people in America prior to 1865 were slaves. Some had been able to purchase or receive their freedom from their owners.

The upheaval and contention over slavery culminated in the Civil War. With the Union victory in 1865, slavery came to an end, but not before it had almost destroyed the Black family unit.

Having no recorded names or written guides, or any other type of written resources, African-Americans pursuing their ancestry face the tremendous challenge of charting their own research course, which could span the United States and perhaps the shores of Africa.

Charting an Uncharted Course. In the pursuit of genealogical research by Black Americans, there is no clear-cut course to follow during and before the Civil War. The traditional course followed by White genealogists differs greatly from the path that Black genealogists are forced to take. They have been assisted immeasurably by the publication of James D. Walker's how-to book on *Black Genealogy*.[1] According to Mr. Walker, researchers using his techniques should have little difficulty tracing their ancestors back to 1870, but beyond that date they will be faced with the horrendous task of locating records during the slavery era.

There is no clear 1-2-3 course to follow for tracing Black ancestry before the Civil War. Elizabeth Clark-Lewis states, "Black genealogy is like a puzzle. You have to go on hunches, clues and when all of a sudden you fit the pieces of the puzzle together, it's emotionally gratifying."[2]

---

[1] James D. Walker, *Black genealogy: How to begin* (Athens, GA: Independent Study, University of Georgia Center for Continuing Education), 1977.

[2] Elizabeth Clark-Lewis is a history professor at Howard University and an expert in oral history.

Part I

A HISTORY OF THE WASHINGTON FAMILY

ISAM/ISOM/ISHAM WASHINGTON (1832-1903)

The war between the North and South had been raging for over three years and the Confederacy was already doomed when Isam Washington enlisted in the Union army. Two days before Christmas, 1864, Isam was mustered in at Paducah, Kentucky as "Substitute (colored) in Lieu of J.S. Petree, a drafted man of Ballard County, KY."[3] The question arises, why would Isam, who was quite possibly married and the father of at least one child, leave his home and family to serve a cause already won? He was not a young man, he gave his age as forty, although other records indicate that he was probably 32 or 33. Existing records yield no answers, only clues. John S. Petree, a doctor, owned land along Shawnee Creek, and Isam lived nearby. Isam's pension records indicate that he was a slave laborer before the war. Did Dr. Petree or his family own Isam? Was he offered land, and perhaps even his freedom, as a reward for his service?

Isam Washington was born in North Carolina in June, 1832.[4] His parents were also born in North Carolina, but the records are silent concerning his family and early childhood. He was probably brought to Ballard County, Kentucky as a slave prior to 1864.

Isam enlisted as a private in the 8th United States Colored Heavy Artillery, Company "L,"[5] a company that had been organized at Paducah, KY on April 26, 1864. It was part of the United States Troops and not a state organization but a national organization.[6] On February 10, 1865, Isam was promoted to the rank of corporal.[7]

In 1865 or early '66, Company "L" was transferred from Oceola, Texas to Victoria, Texas. During the march, Isam's eyes became infected, a

---

[3] Civil War Military Record of Isam Washington's enlistment (copy in possession of the author).

[4] 12th Census of the United States, 1900, Kentucky, Ballard County, ED #2, page 150B.

[5] Civil War Military Records of Isham Washington, National Archives (copy in possession of author).

[6] Thomas Speed, *Union Regiments of Kentucky* (Frankfort, KY: Kentucky Historical Society, 1897), p. 701.

[7] Civil War Military Records of Isham Washington, National Archives (copy in possession of author).

condition that would plague him from time to time for the remainder of his life. Years later, at a hearing before the pension board where he requested that his full pension be restored, he declared of that march:

> I am the claimant in this case: on my march from Oceola, Texas to Victoria, Texas, my eyes became effected [sic] and while in camp on Gaudloupe [sic] Creek, my eyes became very sore and was treated for same by the surgeon Dewing, for some time before I was mustered out at Louisville, KY my eyes had improved some, since I was mustered out of the service I have on two occasions had very sever case of sore eye was not treated by any phisician [sic] used simply treatment one being pith from the safras [sic] bushes and wore goggles and glasses & pads for months or more and then discontue [sic] and in a short time they be come in a same condition again.[8]

Isam was discharged from the army on February 10, 1866[9] at Victoria, Texas, and returned to Ballard County, Kentucky, to join his wife, Rebecca Neal and son, John Ray. He took up farming and appeared on the tax list that same year (1866) as a free negro over 21 years of age.[10]

The following year, January 12, 1867, William Pleasant was born to Isam and Rebecca. During the next few years, four more children arrived, bringing the total to six positively identified children, but there may have been more. Sallie was born January 22, 1869, Mary Jane arrived August 2, 1871, Horace Lee followed on February 17, 1873, and Isam McDaniel was the last child listed, born on May 2, 1875.

In 1872, Isam was listed in the Ballard County Tax Books as a landowner.[11] He obtained fifty-five acres along Humphries Creek but no records exist showing when or from whom he purchased the land as the courthouse located in Wickliff burned in 1880, destroying land and deed records.[12] By 1873 Isam's holdings included his land, one hog, two mules,

---

[8] Civil War Pension Application file of Isam Washington, Ballard Co. Ky., 13 Sept 1890, National Archives, Washington, D.C.

[9] Frederick H. Dyer, *A Compendium of the War of the Rebellion*, Vol. 2 (Dayton, OH: Morningside, 1972), p. 1722.

[10] Ballard County, Ky. Tax Books 1862-1872, Kentucky State Archives.

[11] Ibid., 1872.

[12] Philip M. Cochran, *A Historical Overview of Ballard County* (Frankfort, KY: Kentucky Historical Society, 1978), p. 97.

3,000 pounds of tobacco and 150 bushels of corn.[13] His fortunes and family increased during the following years and in 1876 he appeared in the tax list as a landowner, the father of seven children, and the owner of one horse, two mules, 5,000 pounds of tobacco, 500 bushels of corn and 115 bushels of wheat.

Isam's holdings reached their peak in 1880 when he owned 9,000 pounds of tobacco, 500 bushels of corn, 130 bushels of wheat and six horses and mules valued at $125.00.[14] Based on the large yield of tobacco crops produced yearly, he appears to have been a successful tobacco farmer for many years.

The 1880s brought hardship and tragedy to the Washington family. Isam's recurring eye problems and his rheumatism made it impossible for him to do all the work required on so large a farm. He mortgaged his land and crops consistently during this time and finally lost the land completely (see chart #2).

Second Marriage

Isam's wife, Rebecca died on November 24, 1885,[15] leaving him with five young children still at home. In August of that same year, his neighbor, Woodson Frasier had died,[16] leaving a wife and two children. Isam and Mary Jane Elizabeth (Howell) Frasier were married on December 30, 1885, at the Pleasant Ridge A.M.E. church in Ballard County.[17] The marriage united the two families and brought a happy conclusion to what must otherwise have been a disastrous year.

Isam and Elizabeth (as she preferred to be called) continued to farm and raise their brood of seven children. In December of 1888 a son was born to them whom they named Schooler G.

On June 27, 1890, an act was passed by Congress providing a pension for all Civil War Veterans who had served a minimum of ninety days with an honorable discharge, or who had a permanent physical disability which may or may not have originated in the service. The rate of pay under this

---

[13] Ballard County, Ky. Tax Books 1872-78.

[14] Ibid., 1880.

[15] Civil War Pension Application file of Isam Washington, #831725, Ballard Co., Ky., 21 October 1897, National Archives (photocopy in possession of author).

[16] Ibid., Affidavit, 28 Dec. 1904.

[17] Ibid.

act was graded from $6.00 to $12.00, proportionate to the degree of inability to earn a support, and was not affected by the rank held.[18] Isam's health had continued to deteriorate, and he applied for a pension under this act on September 6, 1890 at Lovelaceville, Ballard Co., Kentucky. He gave his age as 58 and stated that the reason for applying was that he was partially unable to earn a support by reason of eye disease and rheumatism.[19] He apparently received the full pension of $12.00.

The extra funds must have helped the large Washington family, but on May 4, 1895 his pension was reduced from $12.00 to $6.00 per month. Isam was dissatisfied with this reduction and filed a restoration claim with the pension board on August 23, 1897. He stated,

> . . . that he is totally unable to earn a support by reason of disease of eyes, and loss of sight of left eye and rheumatism as alleged in his original application under Act June 27, 1890. He is also afflicted with and disabled by catarrh of head and chronic diarrhoea and resulting piles. He believes that his pension was wrongfully and unjustly reduced from $12.00 per month from May 4, 1895. . . . that he is a pensioner under Certificate No. 831725. . . . Lovelaceville, Ballard, Ky. Signed: Isam Washington.

By November 1, 1897, Isam's pension pay had not been restored. At that time he appeared before the pension board and gave the previously mentioned account of his march to Victoria, Texas and the onset of his eye infection.

Three years passed and there is no evidence that indicates Isam's pension was restored. On May 9, 1900 Congress passed a new act. On August 22, 1900 Isam applied for a pension under the new act. At that time he gave his age as 69 and listed his occupation as a farmer. The document states,

> . . . that he is now unable to earn a support by manual labor by reason of loss of eyesight about three years past. I have a spell of sore eyes at Victoria, Tex. in 1865. . . . That he is a pensioner NEW under Certificate 831725, rate per month $6.00, for PARTIAL INABILITY TO EARN A SUPPORT BY MANUAL LABOR. Witnessed by V.A. Lovelace and Albert Jett, both of Lovelaceville, Ky.

---

[18] Civil War Pension Application file of Isam Washington, Ballard Co., Ky., 13 Sept. 1890, National Archives, Washington, D.C.

[19] Ibid., Declaration for Invalid Pension.

Isam's repeated attempts to obtain a full pension, his own testimony concerning his failing health, and the tax records showing the loss of his property all give us some insight into what life must have been like for the Washington family as they struggled to survive during these difficult years.

It appears that the pension was finally restored to $12.00 per month but the money came too late to help the family. The older children were on their own now, except for John Ray who died probably in 1897, and we find no record of Schooler after the 1900 census so we can assume that he died some time after that year.

In 1900, Isam and Elizabeth were living in Ballard County with their son Schooler and two grandchildren, Artimis and Ezekiel. Sometime after that, Isam and Elizabeth together with their son Mack, his wife and two children, moved across the Ohio River to Illinois where they lived in Massac County, where Mack's wife Arbella originally came from. Isam became a minister in his last years, setting a precedent for three generations of Washingtons to follow. He died in Brookport, Massac County on June 27, 1903, at the age of 73. The cause of death was listed as heart failure. He was buried in a Brookport cemetery on June 28, 1903.[20]

Elizabeth lived on in Massac County for a decade after her husband's death.[21] She died sometime after January 4, 1913.[22]

Genealogical Summary

Isam/Isom/Isham WASHINGTON
    born June 1832 in North Carolina
    married 1: Rebecca NEAL before 1867
        (Rebecca Neal died 24 November 1885 in Ballard Co., Kentucky)
    died 27 June 1903 in Brookport, Massac Co., Illinois

    The 1880 tax records of Ballard Co. KY suggest that Isam and Rebecca Washington had as many as seven or more children. Of this number, six have been positively

---

[20] Register of Death, page 85, Massac Co., Illinois.

[21] 1910 U.S. Census, Massac Co., Illinois, E.D. 70, p. 73.

[22] Civil War Pension file of Elizabeth Washington, widow of Isam, Pensioner ____; document dated 19 February 1913.

identified. All were born in Ballard County according to the tax and pension records.[23]

    i. John Ray
        born 1853 or earlier (since in 1874 he was 21 or older)
        died probably before 1897 in Ballard Co., KY.[24]

    ii. William Pleasant
        born 12 January 1867
        married about 1887 in Ballard Co., KY to Georgia
        died before 1957.[25]

    iii. Sallie
        born 22 January 1869
        married John STAHL 8 March 1886 in Ballard County, KY
        died after April 1957.[26]

---

[23] Isam's pension file dated 21 October 1897 identifies William, [Salvany] Sallie, Mary, Horace L., and Isom as living children of Isom Washington. Isam's mortgage book identifies John Ray as a son of Isom. Possibly Isom was the father of three more children, J. Albert, Ed and Ida Washington, found in Ballard County Records. Right ages to be his children, tax records indicate father of 7 or more children. No other Washington family found living in county 1871-1900; no direct evidence of father-children relationships found.

[24] Birth calculated from tax list, 1874, giving his age as 21 or older. He is noted as the son of Isham Washington who in Oct. 1884 mortgaged his entire crop of tobacco, about 3,000 pounds, to Trewalla Bros. Isham and John Ray gave their marks on the mortgage, since they could not sign their names. See Ballard Co. KY Mortgage Book D, p. 261.

[25] Birth: Isom Civil War Pension File 1897; Marriage: Massac County, Illinois, 1900 U.S. Census, p. 23a; Death: he died prior to his brother Isam Mack D.'s death in April 1957.

[26] Ibid., Birth, 1900 Census, Ballard County, KY, 48; 1910 Census, Ballard Co., KY, ED. No 1, p.5A; Marriage: Marriage Bond, Ballard Co., KY, Marriage Book B, pp. 112-113. April 1957: In Isom Mack D. Washington's obituary she is listed as a surviving sister, living in Paducah, KY.

    iv. Mary Jane
         born 2 August 1871
         no record of a marriage found
         died before April 1957 but was still alive in 1897.[27]

    v. Horace Lee
        born 17 February 1873
        no record of a marriage found
        died before April 1957 but was also alive in 1897.[28]

    vi. Isom McDaniel
         born 2 May 1875
         married Arbella WEEKS 8 August 1896 at Massac County, IL
         died 28 April 1957 in St. Louis, St. Louis Co., MO.

married 2: Mary Jane Elizabeth HOWELL (FRASIER) on 30 December 1885, in Ballard Co., KY.

Mary Jane Elizabeth Howell
    married 1: Woodson FRASIER
    died after 4 January 1913 in Massac Co., IL

Children born to Isam Washington and Mary Jane Elizabeth Howell:

    i. Schooler G.
       born December 1888
       no record found after 1900
       not mentioned in 1897 record file.

    ii. _____

****

---

[27] Ibid., Birth. Marriage: no record found. Death: she died prior to her brother Isom Mack D.'s death in April, 1957.

[28] Ibid., Birth; 1910 Census, Massac County, Illinois, Ed No. 70, p. 73.

ISAM/ISOM McDANIEL (MACK D.) WASHINGTON (1875-1957)

Isam Washington had made a place for himself in the world by the time his youngest son, Isam McDaniel, was born in 1875. That year he owned a 55 acre farm in Ballard County, Kentucky, valued at $400.00. He also owned one horse, value $20.00, two mules, value $100.00, three cattle, value $560.00, six children between 6-20 years of age, one hog, 3400 pounds of tobacco, two tons of hay, 200 bushels of corn, and 137 bushels of wheat. The Ballard County Tax Lists show that father Isam had risen from slavery to landowner and successful tobacco farmer in just one generation.

Isam McDaniel, the youngest son of Isam and Rebecca (Neal) Washington, joined the family on May 2, 1875.[29] He was named for his father and called "Mack," the name by which he would be known throughout his life. There was much to be done on so large a farm and Mack probably worked alongside his older brothers and sisters, learning from them and from his parents during his early years.

When Mack was ten years old, his mother died and his father remarried. His stepmother, Elizabeth, brought two more children to the family, making the total of children at home seven. Three years later, when Mack was 13, his half-brother, Schooler, was born.

By the time Mack reached his teens, life was harder. His father had lost the farm and was now a tenant farmer suffering from rheumatism and failing eyesight. Mack's brothers were marrying and leaving home, and Mack was assuming more responsibility for the running of the farm.

When he was 21, Mack married Arbella Weeks, from Brooklyn, Massac Co., Illinois. Since Massac County is just across the Ohio River from Ballard County, Mack didn't have to travel far to find his bride. They were married at Metropolis, Massac County, on August 8, 1896.[30]

Like Mack, Arbella lost a parent when she was very young. Her father, Smith Weeks, died shortly after her birth on April 29, 1878 in Mississippi

---

[29] Birth: Isam/Isham Civil War Pension file, 1897.

[30] Marriage: Marriage Register of Massac County, IL, file #3822. Death: Death Certificate, Illinois State file #32328 (copy in writer's possession).

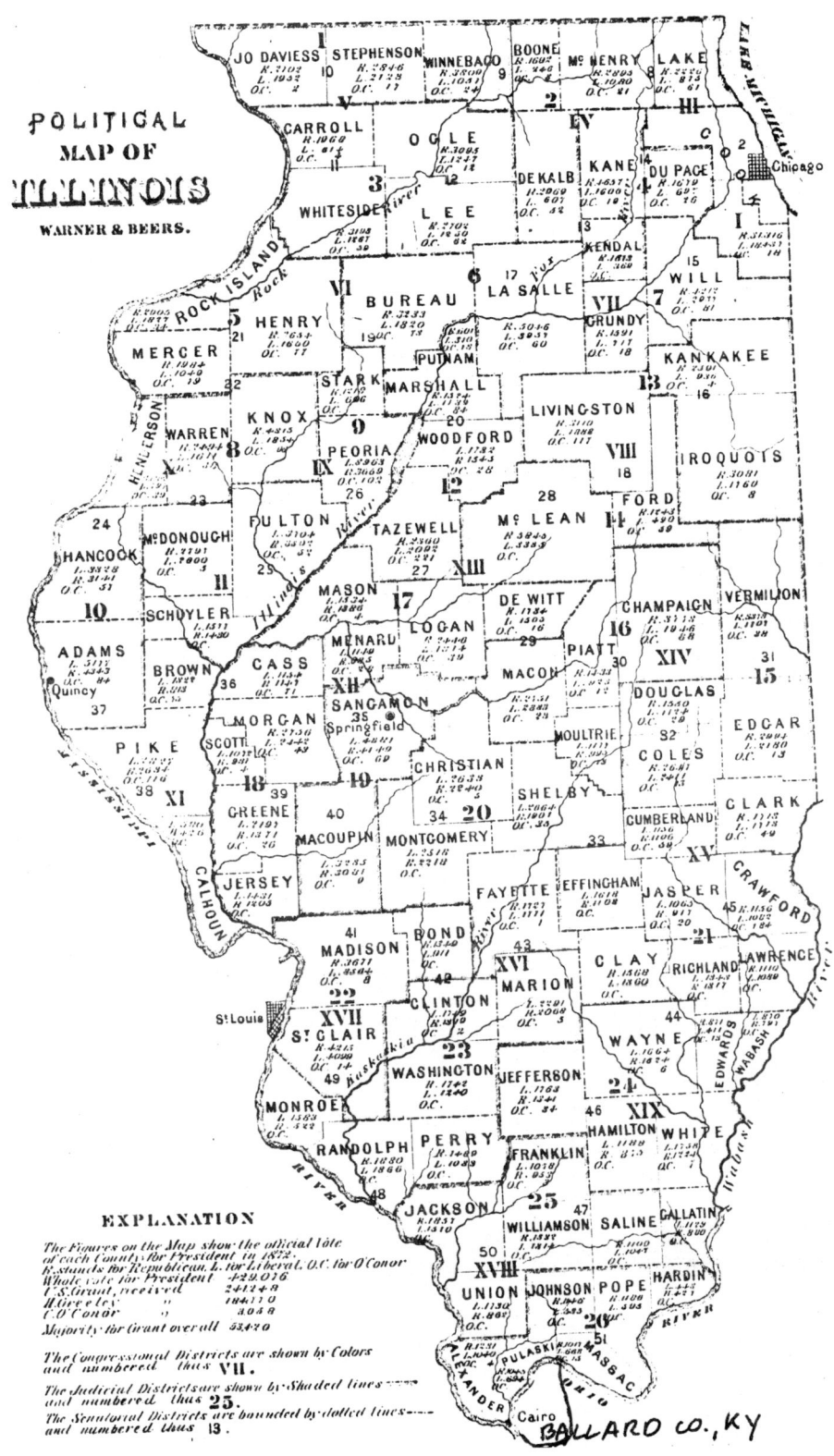

Figure 1. **1872 county map for the state of Illinois (with Ballard County, Kentucky, sketched in).**

15

County, Arkansas.[31] Her mother, Elizabeth Robinson Weeks married Sep Hamilton and he became the only father she and her older sister, Lula, ever knew. In fact, Arbella often gave her maiden name as Hamilton.

Sep and Elizabeth raised a large family. Joseph, Sep's son, was eight years older than Lula, and ten years older than Arbella. One daughter and four sons were born to Sep and Elizabeth, making eight children in all.

Soon after Mack and Arbella were married, they moved to Lovelaceville, Ballard County, where they rented a home next door to Mack's parents, Isam and Elizabeth. Mack began farming for himself, as well as helping his father.[32] Their first two children were born here; Roy L. arriving on April 12, 1897, and Elizabeth (Lizzie) in October, 1899.[33] Lizzie was appropriately named for both of her grandmothers.

Move to Illinois

Soon after the turn of the century, the Washingtons made a decision that would affect not only their own lives and that of their descendants, but also the lives of millions of Chicagoans in years to come. Isam was now nearly blind and his painful rheumatism prevented him from being much help on the farm. Isam and Elizabeth were responsible for three dependent children: Schooler, their own son; and two grandchildren, Artimis and Ezekiel. Isam was still waiting for the government to restore his pension, and Mack had a dream of becoming a minister. Arbella's family lived just across the river in Massac Co.; perhaps they could help. So it was that Mack, Arbella, Isam and Elizabeth packed up children, grandchildren and whatever possessions they could carry, left Kentucky, their family home for nearly forty years, and moved to Illinois.

In Illinois, Isam and Mack both became ministers of the African Methodist Episcopal (A.M.E.) Church in Brookport. At some point, Mack's brother, William, joined them in the ministry. It is not known where or when the Washingtons received their training for the ministry, but many church buildings stand today as silent testaments to the work accomplished by Reverend Mack Washington.

While they were living in Brookport, Isam passed away and a year later, Mack and Arbella's third child, Booker T., was born. He came into

---

[31] Birth: 1880 U.S. Census, Brooklyn, Massac Co., IL ED 62, sheet 558, June 1880 (calculated from census record, Massac Co. Marriage Register).

[32] 1900 U.S. Census, Ballard Co., KY ED #2, p. 151A.

[33] Ibid.

Isam McDaniel (Mack D.) Washington, Harold Washington's grandfather.

the world on September 20, 1904.[34] Eleven years later, the family was living in Lawrence County, Illinois where Mack performed the duties of pastor at both Lawrenceville and Pinkstaff.

Mack and Arbella's home in Pinkstaff became the site of an event important enough to be reported in the local newspaper. The Lawrenceville *Republican* of 11 November, 1915 reports as follows:

> Last night shortly after retiring, Reverent Washington was suddenly aroused from his slumber by a knock at the door. On opening the door to investigate, a crowd of people rushed in each with a large package. Of course the surprised minister knew what this meant after a while. This is what is known as a surprise pound party. Those who brought pounds were Mr. and Mrs. Joseph Tann, Mr. and Mrs. Clingman, Mr. and Mrs. Samuel Casey, Mr. and Mrs. Wm. Anderson, Mr. and Mrs. Joseph Wimberly, Mr. and Mrs. Clifton Goins, Mrs. Elihu Anderson, Blanch Portee, Mr. and Mrs. Wm. Tompkins, Mr. and Mrs. Jeff Walls, Mr. and Mrs. Curtis [?], Mrs. Harl Portee, Messrs. Troy Anderson, Lewis Harris, Doc Anderson, Mr. and Mrs. Robert Portee, Mr. and Mrs. Benj. Anderson, Mr. and Mrs. James Morris and Misses Evelyn and Martha Morris. Reverend Washington fully enjoyed such a surprise as this and did not feel in the least offended.[35]

Carl R. Curry told me, "After talking to the old-timers we found that a 'pound party' was when everyone brought a pound of various items of food (flour, sugar, meat, etc.). The Morris people listed above were my ancestors. My mother was a Morris. Most of the people above have descendants living around here now."[36] The pound party may have been a way for Mack's parishioners to show their affection and respect for their minister.

Mack had been instrumental in raising money and then building St. James Church in Lawrenceville. The first services were held there on

---

[34] Division of Vital Records, Massac Co., IL, Certificate of Birth Book, p. 3.

[35] Lawrenceville *Republican*, 11 November 1915.

[36] Carl R. Curry, Rt. 1, Bridgeport Illinois, 3 October 1988.

Figure 2. St. James A.M.E. Church, 1988.

August 10, 1916, with Reverend I. Mack D. Washington officiating.[37] St. James Church still stands on the corner of 11th and Ash St. in Lawrenceville.[38]

Ministerial Career

Mack served as minister in the Pinkstaff Circuit for many years. The circuit consisted of Bethel Church at Pinkstaff and St. James Church at Lawrenceville, with Bethel being the Mother Church. In the early 1960s, Bethel A.M.E. Church was closed. All its members currently attend St. James or other area churches.[39] St. James A.M.E. Church is now the only A.M.E. church in Lawrence County.

From Lawrence County, Mack and Arbella moved to Decatur, Illinois, where Mack served as Pastor of St. Peter's A.M.E. Church.[40] In 1922 they lived at 540 Greenwood Avenue with their daughter Elizabeth and son Booker.[41]

In Decatur, Mack again directed his efforts towards raising money for a new church. His goal was achieved in 1927 when the new St. Peter's A.M.E. Church was completed. A history of Macon County, Illinois, compiled by M.E. Richmond, states: "The present St. Peter's A.M.E. Church, pictured, located on the west side of Greenwood Avenue, was erected in 1927. Reverend J.H. Sydes started the building fund, Reverend I.M.D. Washington added to it, and Reverend R.H. Hackley completed the building project."[42] This information supported a letter written to the writer by Mrs. Robert Senor of Springfield, Illinois, in which she states, "During his lifetime Rev. Washington was known for building churches and raising money."[43] In 1930, Mack and Arbella were still in Decatur, residing at 1955 North Church Street with their son, Booker, and his wife, Marie.

---

[37] Lawrenceville *Republican*, 10 August 1916.

[38] Lawrence County Genealogical Society, "History of St. James A.M.E. Church," (September, 1988), Lawrenceville, Illinois.

[39] Ibid.

[40] Decatur Genealogical Society, "City Directory 1922," Decatur, Illinois.

[41] Ibid., 1925.

[42] M.E. Richmond, "Centennial History of Macon County, 1935," Decatur Genealogical Society, Decatur, Ill., p. 333.

[43] Letter to the writer from Mrs. Robert Senor of Springfield, Illinois, dated 10 February 1984.

By 1934, the Washingtons had moved again, this time to Springfield, Illinois. Mack's new assignment was to St. John's A.M.E. Church. The family disappears from the Springfield city directories between 1936 and 1947, but reappears in 1948, with Mack shown as pastor of Grace Methodist Church. In 1950, it is believed that Mack and Arbella were living in the small town of Carrier Mills, Illinois. They returned to their home in Springfield in 1951 and were living there when Arbella died on July 1, 1952.[44] Arbella's obituary appeared in *Illinois State Journal*, July 2, 1952, p. 34:

> Mrs. Arbella Washington, of 1423 E. Carpenter St., died at 9:30 p.m. yesterday at the residence after an extended illness. She was 73 years old. Mrs. Washington had been a resident of Springfield since 1947. She is survived by her husband, Rev. I.M.D. Washington; two sons, Attorney Roy L., Chicago, and Booker T., St. Louis, Mo.; a daughter, Mrs. Elizabeth Johnson, Detroit, Mich.; three grandchildren, Mrs. Geneva Watson, city, and Roy L. Jr. and Harold Washington, Chicago; five great-grandchildren [Travis Lercy Watson, Bertha Maria Watson, William Arnold Watson, Richard Allen Watson, Francine Louise Watson] and other relatives. Remains were taken to the Carpenter Funeral Home. Funeral arrangements are incomplete.

Arbella was buried at Oak Ridge Cemetery in Springfield. Mack continued on in the family home but his remaining years were sad ones. His oldest son, Roy, died on November 7, 1953, and his daughter, Elizabeth, died less than four months later.[45] They were both in their fifties.

In 1955, Mack's grandchildren took him to live with his only surviving son, Booker, in St. Louis, Missouri. Here he died on April 28, 1957,[46] "a broken-hearted man after his wife passed," according to the previously mentioned letter from Mrs. Senor.

An excerpt from Mack's Last Will and Testament, which he wrote on March 3, 1954, designates Booker as his only remaining heir: ". . . After the payment of such funeral expenses and debts, I give, devise and

---

[44] Birth and death information from death certificate, Illinois State file #32328.

[45] Birth and death information from copies of death certificates in possession of writer.

[46] Birthplace and death information from death certificate, Missouri State file #15429.

bequeath all my real and personal property to my only son, BOOKER T. WASHINGTON of 4047 Finney Avenue, St. Louis, Missouri, whose phone number is 5681."[47]

Reverend I.M.D. Washington's obituary appeared in *Illinois State Journal*, 30 April 1957, p. 3:

> Reverend I.M.D. Washington, St. Louis MO., former pastor of St. John's A.M.E. Church, died yesterday at the home of his son, Booker Washington, in St. Louis. He is survived by a sister, Mrs. Sally Stahl, Paducah, Ky.; his son, of St. Louis; two grandsons and seven great-grandchildren. Funeral services will be held at 7:30 p.m. Wednesday at the Gates Funeral Home in St. Louis.

Genealogical Summary

Isam McDaniel (Mack D.) WASHINGTON
    born 2 May 1875 in Ballard Co., Kentucky
    married Arbella WEEKS 8 August 1896 in Massac Co., IL
    died 28 April 1957 in St. Louis, St. Louis Co., MO.

Arbella WEEKS
    born 29 April 1878 in Mississippi Co., Arkansas
    died 1 July 1952 in Springfield, Sangamon Co., IL.

Children of Isam McDaniel Washington and Arbella Weeks:[48]

  i. Roy L.
     born 12 April 1897 at Lovelaceville, Ballard Co., KY
     married 1: Bertha JONES 29 July 1916
     married 2: Arlene JACKSON 30 June 1933
     died 7 November 1953 in Chicago, Cook Co., IL.

  ii. Elizabeth "Lizzie"
     born October 1899 at Lovelaceville, Ballard Co., KY
     married Nelson JOHNSON
     died 25 February 1954 at Detroit, Wayne Co., MI.[49]

---

[47] Will. Book 57, page 12, filed 12 July 1957, Springfield, Sangamon County, Illinois.

[48] 1900 and 1910 Census Records.

[49] Death Certificate. Michigan State file #6676.

iii. Booker T.
   born 21 September 1904 at Brookport, Massac Co., IL
   married Marie [?] EMMETT after 1924
   died 14 July 1962 at St. Louis, St. Louis Co., MO.[50]

* * * * * * *

ROY WASHINGTON (1897-1953)

Roy's parents, Mack and Arbella Weeks Washington, were newly married and living in Lovelaceville, Ballard County, Kentucky when Roy was born on April 12, 1897.[51] He was the oldest of three children and his father was a tenant farmer with a dream of becoming a minister. When he was still very young he moved with his parents, grandparents and sister, Lizzie, to Brookport, Massac County, Illinois where his brother, Booker T., was born in 1904.[52]

Roy was fortunate that his early years were spent in close proximity to both sets of grandparents. Although his grandfather, Isam, died when Roy was only six, his step-grandmother, Elizabeth, lived until he was at least 16 and must have been a strong influence on the growing boy.

Roy's father became a minister in the A.M.E. Church and the family moved about as Mack received assignments to various churches. In 1916 they were living in Pinkstaff, Lawrence County, Illinois and Roy was attending Lawrenceville Township High School in Lawrenceville.

While still in high school, Roy fell in love with Bertha Jones who lived in Carrier Mills, a nearby town. He was 19 and she was 18. When they decided to marry, it was necessary for Roy's father to give his consent because Roy was still a minor. They were married on July 29, 1916 with Reverend I.M.D. Washington performing the marriage ceremony.

---

[50] Birth information from birth records, Massac County, Illinois Vital Records; death information from Death Certificate, Missouri State file #62 029279. Copy in possession of writer; marriage date calculated from lack of spouse's name in 1924 city directory.

[51] Death Certificate #80618, 1953, Chicago, Cook County, Illinois Vital Records.

[52] 1910 U.S. Census, White County, Illinois, E.D. 136, p. 62. Death Certificate, Booker T. Washington, Missouri State file #62 029279. Massac County, Illinois Certificate of Birth, p. 3.

Roy Washington, Harold Washington's father.

Bertha Jones Washington, Harold Washington's mother.

MARRIAGE LICENSE.

The People of the State of Illinois, County of

To any Person Legally Authorized to Solemnize Marriage—GREETING:

Marriage may be Celebrated Between Mr. Roy Washington of Pinkstaff in the County of Lawrence and State of Illinois of the age of 19 years, and Miss Bertha Jones of Carrier Mills in the County of Saline and State of Illinois of the age of 18 years, the Father of the said minor having given assent to said Marriage.

Witness, H. E. Wills County Clerk, and the seal of said County, at his office in Harrisburg in said County, this 29 day of July A. D. 1916

H. E. Wills
County Clerk.

STATE OF ILLINOIS,
Saline County, } ss.

I, I. M. W. Washington Minister hereby certify that Mr. Roy Washington and Miss Bertha Jones were united in Marriage by me at Carrier Mills in the County of Saline and State of Illinois, on the 29 day of July A. D. 1916

I. M. D. Washington
Minister.

Figure 3. Marriage license of Roy Washington and Bertha Jones.

After his marriage, Roy completed his high school education, graduating from Lawrenceville High in 1917 or later (see Figure 4).

At the same time Roy was finishing high school, Bertha was busy starting their family. Their first son, Roy Jr., was born in Carrier Mills, Saline County, Illinois in 1916 and their daughter, Geneva, was born in 1918.

With high school behind him, Roy took Bertha and their two children to Cook County where he enrolled in Chicago's Kent College of Law. Their third child, Edward, was born in Chicago on October 19, 1920,[53] and Harold arrived on April 15, 1922,[54] the same year that Roy graduated from law school.[55] He passed the Illinois State Bar examination on April 12, 1923.

Divorce and Remarriage

The hard years seemingly behind them, Roy and Bertha's marriage did not survive the pressures caused by Roy's schooling and four small children. Roy and Bertha were divorced in 1928, with Roy receiving custody of the children.[56] Bertha later remarried and had seven more children. Roy Jr. and Geneva were sent to southern Illinois to live with their grandparents, while Edward and Harold remained with their father. Roy and the children moved into the home of his sister, Lizzie Johnson, on the near South Side in Chicago's third ward,[57] where Roy became active in the Democratic party, serving as a precinct captain.

Many years later Harold would say of this time with his father: "I was very fortunate. My father was my role model. For many years he was not only my father, he was my mother . . . and he came home every night, put his feet under the table and had dinner with me."[58]

---

[53] Birth Certificate #42932, Chicago, Cook Co., IL Vital Records.

[54] Birth Certificate #15512, 1922, Chicago, Cook Co., IL Vital Records.

[55] John Marshall Law School, *Alumni Directory*, (1899-1939), Chicago, Illinois, p. 69.

[56] Divorce Decree #477276, July term 1928, Chicago, Cook County, Illinois. *Roy L. Washington v. Bertha Washington*.

[57] Dempsey J. Travis, *Harold--The People's Mayor* (Chicago: Urban Research Press, Inc., 1989), p. 3.

[58] Interview with Harold Washington, *Chicago Sun-Times*, April 10, 1983, p. 4.

Figure 4. Photograph of Roy Washington and classmates.

Five years after his divorce, Roy married for the second time. His bride was Arlene Jackson, a teacher of music (it was said) from Kansas City. They were married on June 30, 1933.[59] Roy continued the study of law and in 1937 he was awarded his second law degree from John Marshall Law School in Chicago.[60]

Career

Roy accomplished another lifetime goal on September 20, 1942 when he was appointed Evangelist of the A.M.E. Church by Bishop J.A. Gregg. This made three generations of ministers in the Washington family.

At the same time, his career as an attorney was on the rise. In 1942 he became a member of the Illinois State Bar Association, and was admitted to practice law in the U.S. Supreme Court in 1945.

Roy also had political aspirations. In 1947 he was an aldermanic candidate for the third ward where he had lived and practiced law for years. He ran on the following platform:

RID DISTRICT OF FIRE TRAPS...
RID THE DISTRICT OF RAT INFESTED BASEMENTS...
IMPROVE BAD LIGHTING SYSTEM...
IMPROVE SEWAGE SYSTEM TO DRAIN WASTE FROM STREETS...
SECURE MORE PLAYGROUNDS FOR OUR CHILDREN...
CLEANER STREETS AND ALLEYS...
BETTER TRANSPORTATION...
THIRD WARD VOTERS!
GET ON THE BANDWAGON AND SUPPORT A FIGHTER
BE WITH THE WINNER
YOU DESERVE THE BEST
ROY L. WASHINGTON
FOR ALDERMAN THIRD WARD

---

[59] Marriage License #1374161, Chicago, Cook County, Illinois Record Office.

[60] John Marshall Law School, *Alumni Directory* (1899-1939), Chicago, Illinois, p. 69.

Roy lost the aldermanic election of February 25, 1947. The following month, his son Edward, who was only 26, died[61] and was buried in Lincoln Cemetery.[62]

At the height of his career as an attorney, Roy was stricken with cancer of the pancreas. He died on November 7, 1953 at the age of 56.[63] Roy had been practicing law in Chicago for more than twenty years. He was survived by his widow, Arlene; two sons, Roy Jr. and Harold; his daughter, Geneva Watson; his father, Reverend Mack Washington; a sister, Elizabeth Johnson and a brother, Booker T.[64] He was buried in Lincoln Cemetery on November 10, 1953.[65]

Genealogical Summary

Roy L. WASHINGTON
    born 12 April 1897 at Lovelaceville, Ballard Co., KY
    married 1: Bertha JONES 29 July 1916 at Carrier Mills, Saline
       Co., IL
    married 2: Arlene JACKSON 30 June 1933 at Chicago, Cook Co., IL
    died 7 November 1953 at Chicago, Cook Co., IL

    Children of Roy L. Washington and Bertha Jones:

    i. Roy L. Jr.
       born 1916 at Carrier Mills, Saline Co., IL

    ii. Geneva
       born 1918 in Saline Co., IL
       married Francis WATSON

---

[61] Death Certificate #7287, 1947, Chicago, Cook County, Illinois, Vital Records.

[62] Headstone Inscription, Lincoln Cemetery, 123 S. Kedzie Avenue, Blue Island, Illinois, Lot 154, Section 8.

[63] Death Certificate #80618-1953, Chicago, Cook County, Illinois, Vital Records.

[64] *Chicago Daily Defender*, 7 November 1953, pages 1-3, burial announcement of Roy L. Washington. Microfilm, Woodson Public Library, Chicago, Illinois.

[65] Headstone, Lincoln Cemetery, 123 S. Kedzie Avenue, Blue Island, Illinois, Lot 154, Section 8.

iii. Edward Glen
   born 10 October 1920 at Chicago, Cook Co., IL
   died 6 March 1947 at Chicago, Cook Co., IL

iv. Harold Lee
   born 15 April 1922 at Chicago, Cook Co., IL
   married Nancy Dorothy FINCH 22 July 1942 at Chicago,
      Cook Co., IL
   died 25 November 1987 at Chicago, Cook Co., IL

* * * * * * *

HAROLD LEE WASHINGTON (1922-1987)

Politics was in Harold Washington's blood. The youngest son of a Democratic Precinct Captain on Chicago's South Side, Harold learned the ropes at an early age. He was working in the precinct around 44th Street and Michigan Avenue when he was only 13, absorbing all that his father could teach him.

Harold was born on April 15, 1922 in Cook County Hospital on the West Side of Chicago. He was the third son and fourth child of Roy L. and Bertha Jones Washington, and at the time of his birth, his parents were living on the South Side of Chicago at 3341 South Prairie Street.[66]

When Harold was six years old, his parents were divorced. His oldest brother, Roy, and sister, Geneva, went to live with grandparents while Harold and his brother, Edward, moved with their father into the home of Aunt "Lizzie" Johnson, Roy's sister.

Soon after the breakup of the family, Harold and Edward were taken out of public school and sent to St. Benedict the Moor Grammar School in Milwaukee, Wisconsin (see Figure 5). According to a letter to the author from St. Benedict's school, Edward spent two years there while Harold attended the school for four years, from September 1928 to June 1932. When he left St. Benedict's, he returned to his home in Chicago where he completed his elementary education at Forrestville Elementary School.

In June, 1933, Roy remarried, this time to Arlene Jackson, and once again the Washingtons were a complete family. Harold's teenage years were spent on Chicago's South Side where he worked in the precinct with his

---

[66] Birth Certificate, Illinois State Board of Health, File #15512, Chicago, Cook County, Illinois Vital Records.

RECORD CARD

ST. BENEDICT THE MOOR BOARDING SCHOOL

BOARDER

DAY SCHOLAR

NAME Harold Lee Washington

ADDRESS 4305 Vincennes Ave. Chgo.

BORN 15 OF April 1922

GRADE 1

FORMERLY AT Public

SCHOOL Chicago, Illinois

BAPTIZED OF 19

IN CHURCH

PRESENT HEALTH CONDITION OK.

DOCTOR

REFERENCE

ENTERED Sept. 4-28 LEFT 6-8-32

TUITION TO BE PAID $ 40.00

MUSIC $ None

NAME OF FATHER Roy L. Washington

ADDRESS 4305 Vincennes, Chgo

NAME OF MOTHER Bertha Jones.

ADDRESS Unknown

REMARKS

19....... 19.......	SEPT.	OCT.	NOV.	DEC.	JAN.	FEB.	MAR.	APR.	MAY	JUNE	JULY	AUG.
Tuition	Same as Edward's											
Music												

Figure 5. **St. Benedict's School record of Harold L. Washington.**

father and delivered newspapers with his best friend, John P. Cheefus, who later became a Deputy Sheriff.

After elementary school, Harold entered DuSable High School on the South Side, named in honor of Jean Point DuSable, a Black man who was one of the first settlers in Chicago in the early 19th century. While in high school Harold was active in sports. He won the 120-yard high hurdles in a city-wide track competition during his second year at DuSable; he became a proficient boxer; and he played third base as a member of the "Raggedy Nine," a neighborhood baseball team whose name "was inspired by the unsightly appearance of the team members, many of whose families were too poor to afford baseball T-shirts and caps."[67]

In March, 1939, Harold left DuSable. From July 8th to December 22nd he was one of the two and a half million young men who participated in the Civilian Conservation Corps (C.C.C.), an agency authorized and set up by the government as part of the New Deal Program of 1933 to hire unemployed young men. The C.C.C. provided Harold with a place to live — it was an army-like setting — as well as $8.00 a month in cash and $22.00 a month for his parents. On July 8, 1939, he took the oath of agreement to serve six months and was sent to Company 570, Manistee National Forest, Newaygo County, Camp Bitely, Michigan.[68] The work program of the camp consisted of various projects: reforestation, graveling truck trails, constructing campgrounds and surveying. Harold was assigned to reforestation. His job included raising pine seedlings, making charcoal for filters used in operating a stone quarry which produced road rock, making wooden signs for national parks and clearing underbrush from the forest. The Manistee National Forest camp boasted a baseball team as well as opportunities for basketball, ping pong, wrestling and boxing. Harold honed his boxing skills and it is reported that he won fifty out of sixty fights while he was there.

On October 3, 1939, Harold was transferred to Camp Stockton, in Stockton, Illinois, where he was assigned to Company 610 as a laborer in Soil Erosion. On December 22, 1939, after six months in the C.C.C., Harold was honorably discharged and he returned to Chicago where he moved in with his father.[69]

After his discharge from the C.C.C., Harold worked at several jobs, including a stint at Wilson and Co., the same company in which his father

---

[67] *Dollars and Sense Magazine*, "Coming of Age on South Indiana Avenue" (Chicago: National Publications Sales Agency, 1983), p. 8.

[68] Civilian Conservation Corps Records, Individual Record Serial No. CC 6-269313-Illinois, National Archives, Washington, D.C.

[69] Ibid.

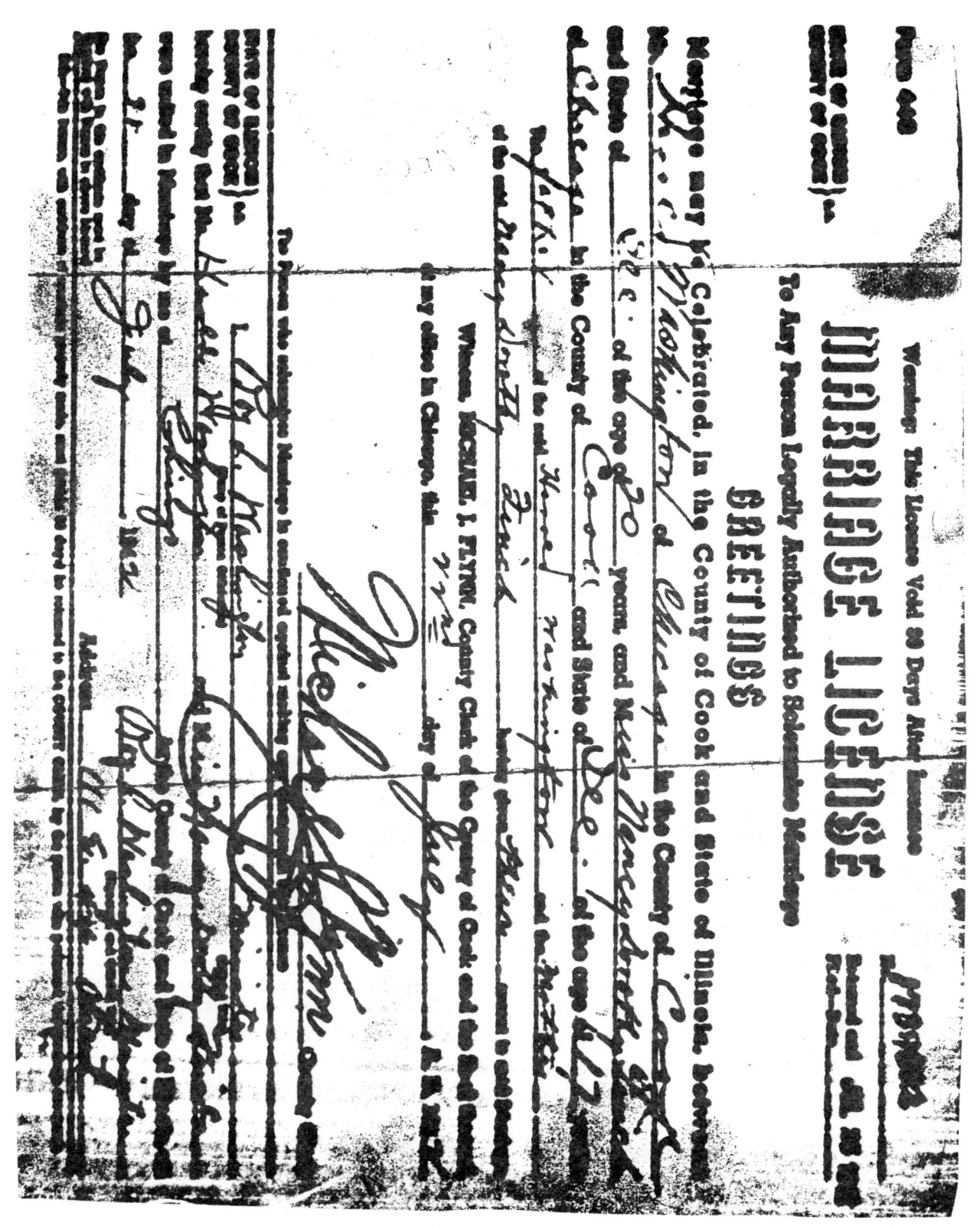

Figure 6. Marriage license of Harold Washington and Nancy Dorothy Finch.

had worked years before while he attended law school at night. It is said that in the spring of 1942 Harold passed a Civil Service Exam and became a clerk in the Chicago office of the U.S. Treasury Department.

Harold married his neighborhood sweetheart, Nancy Dorothy Finch, on July 22, 1942 in Chicago.[70] The wedding ceremony was performed by his father, Reverend Roy L. Washington, who was a minister as well as a lawyer. The wedding took place in his father's home at 111 East 44th St.[71] Harold was twenty and she was seventeen at the time of their marriage (see Figure 6).

Army Service

Seven months earlier, the United States had declared war on Japan after the bombing of Pearl Harbor. Harold and Nancy had seven months together before Harold was called to active duty in the U.S. Army on February 8, 1943.[72]

Harold was processed into the army at Fort Custer, near Battle Creek, Michigan on February 15, 1943. He was sent immediately to Hammerfield, California for basic training and then assigned to the 1887th Engineer Aviation Battalion at March Field, California. He remained with this battalion for the duration of his service in the U.S. Army.[73] The 1887th Battalion remained at March Field for a year, training men to build bridges, repair roads and construct landing strips and mine fields.

While at March Field, Pvt. Washington attended Camouflage and Soil Mechanic School. After advanced training, he was assigned as a Physics Laboratory Technician. His job included supervising physical testing and experimental work in military equipment for soil analysis tests.[74] After three months of active duty, Pvt. Washington was promoted to the rank of

---

[70] Marriage License File #1739602.

[71] Ibid.

[72] Army of the United States, Discharge Record of Harold L. Washington, #36 795331, Personnel Records Center, St. Louis, Mo.

[73] "The History of the 1887th Engineer Aviation Battalion," National Archives and Records Center, Washington, D.C.

[74] Army of the United States, Discharge Records of Harold L. Washington, #36 795331, Personnel Records Center, St. Louis, Mo.

Figure 7. Photograph of Pvt. Harold Washington (1943).

corporal. He served as a corporal for eight months before being promoted to sergeant.[75]

The 1887th Battalion was preparing for combat duty. The United States was at war on two fronts, in Europe with Germany and with the Japanese in the Pacific Islands. On January 17, 1944, Major Charles V. Brown was assigned as commander of the 1887th Battalion and, unknown to the troops, a date had been set for the battalion to do overseas duty. The men spent February and March building hundreds of crates and filling them with supplies in preparation for their voyage. In April Harold and his comrades left March Field, which had been their home for a year, and boarded a troop train which took them, in about a week, to Camp Patrick Henry, Virginia, where they awaited orders for an overseas assignment. Meanwhile, their destination was changed and on April 12, 1944, they were transported, again by train, to Greenville Army Air Base, near Greenville, South Carolina. For many of the men, this was their first exposure to the heart of the South.

Late in April, the unit received moving orders. Telegrams were dispatched to the men on furlough, and supplies were packed. On May 1, 1944, the 1887th Battalion embarked on another cross-country tour, their destination Fort Lawton, Seattle, Washington. On May 13, 1944, the battalion received its sailing orders and boarded the *U.S.S. Grant*, sailing the next morning for an unknown destination. After eight days at sea on the Pacific, the *Grant* reached Honolulu, Hawaii. The battalion's campsite was on the Island of Oahu near the small village of Kahuku, just north of the prominent Mormon Temple at Laie which had served as a landmark for the Japanese planes as they attacked Pearl Harbor in December, 1941. For three months Harold and his comrades received intensive training in manning rubber boats, loading and unloading LSTs (landing-ship transports), and scaling rope ladders.

On August 6, 1944, the 1887th, ready at last to begin the mission for which they had originally been activated, boarded a ship and two days later left Hawaii. On August 27 the battalion arrived at Tulagi, in the Solomon Islands. Then, on September 4, a convoy including the 1887th left the Solomons, again destination unknown.

On September 12, the men were assembled and given the long awaited information. The task force, including the 1887th, was to bombard and invade two of the western Caroline Islands, Pelelieu and Anguar, which were occupied by the Japanese. The mission of the 1887th Engineer Aviation Battalion to which Sergeant Washington was assigned was to help pave the way for the invasion by building a bomber landing strip on Anguar. Twenty days after the battalion, along with the 1884th Battalion, began construction on the runway, it was operational. For putting this

---

[75] Ibid.

runway into service in such an incredibly short time, the two battalions received the Meritorious Service Unit Award.

The invasion on Anguar lasted until mid-October, 1944. Approximately 1200 Japanese were killed or captured in the invasion. Afterwards, the 1887th Battalion remained on the island, building and otherwise improving living conditions. Before the unit left, they had completed several major projects: a runway, two taxiways and one transient hotel ready for use, as well as scores of other jobs that needed to be done. On February 27, 1945, the men of the 1887th boarded the *U.S.S. Johnson* and left Anguar for the island of Guam. On the morning of February 15, 1945, the *Johnson* landed at Guam. Here the men of the 1887th remained until they were demobilized later in 1945.

Sgt. Harold Washington wrote, as part of an introduction to a compiled history of the 1887th Engineer Aviation Battalion:

> This history of the 1887th Engineer Aviation Battalion may be considered the result of a common effort rather than the achievement of any one person or small group of persons. It is primarily a document of reminiscent value to us, who have lived its pages; but there is another purpose for its having been conceived and compiled. That purpose is to acquaint you, who may not know us, with the achievements that we have accomplished, and of which we are justly proud.
>
> To deal minutely with each man at work and at play, would have been an unafforded time and space consuming task; we have included as many as our talents and resources would allow. Suffice it to say that for each man depicted, and for each incident listed in this history, hundreds of others had to precede it to make our work possible, and hundreds of others had to follow to insure its success.
>
> Our battalion is repetitious of hundreds of others, in that it consists of men from all walks of life, and from sundry geographical positions within our beloved United States; called together for the common purpose of bringing and securing the perpetuation of peace to our country. It is different from other battalions in one all-important aspect — it is our battalion.

> V-J Day has come and gone, and though our work continues, we have found time to record the infinitesimal part that we played to make that day possible.
>
> Harold Washington
Guam, October 1945[76]

Harold Washington left Guam on January 1, 1946 and arrived in the United States on January 14. He was discharged at the Camp Grant, Illinois Separation Center on January 20, 1946.[77] He left the military service with an impressive record. Rising through the ranks from private to first sergeant, he received three Overseas Service Bars, an American Campaign Medal, an Asiatic Pacific Theater Ribbon, a Good Conduct Medal, and a World War II Victory Medal.

Six months after his discharge, Harold was listed on the roster of graduates at DuSable High School.[78] Military records indicate that Harold graduated from DuSable High School before entering the U.S. Army; however, the writer was unable to find any evidence to support this claim. Therefore he must have graduated in 1946 (see Figure 9).

Harold continued his education at Roosevelt University (called Roosevelt College at the time) under the G.I. Bill. At Roosevelt he majored in Political Science. He served as president of his senior class and the student council. He graduated with a Bachelor of Arts degree in 1949.[79]

In 1950, Harold and Nancy's marriage ended in divorce.[80] Of the eight years they had been married, they had been apart almost four years while Harold was in the service. They had no children.

Harold's education did not stop with a B.A. degree. He entered Northwestern University Law School and earned a law degree, like his

---

[76] "The History of the 1887th Engineer Aviation Battalion," National Archives and Records Center, Washington, D.C.

[77] Army of the United States, Discharge Records of Harold L. Washington, #36 795331, Personnel Records Center, St. Louis, Mo.

[78] "Graduating List," June 26, 1946, DuSable High School. Proceedings Board of Education, City of Chicago, July 11, 1945-June 26, 1946, p. 1416. Board of Education Library, Chicago, Ill.

[79] Roosevelt University Alumni Directory (1949), Chicago, Ill.

[80] Divorce Decree #14428, 25 February 1950, Chicago Heights, Ill.

Figure 8. **Photograph of Sgt. Harold Washington (1945).**

Walsh, Richard Ray
Wendt, James Joseph
Wenckus, Burton
Werderits, Frand G.
Werner, Edward F.
Wielgus, Edwin
Wikarski, Henry Nick
Wildey, Donald A.
Wilhausen, Edward O.
Wilk, Henry Joseph
Wilkosz, Edward E.
Williams, John Dallas
Wilson, Charles W.
Wiseman, Algar W.
Witek, Leonard W.
Wojdyla, Norbert Paul
Wolf, Donald E.
Wolf, Gilbert
Wojciechowski, Anton W.
Wolinski, Ralph Stanley
Woodfork, Hartford
Woods, Donald Dean
Woodward, David S.
Young, Freeman
Zahl, John F.
Zaleski, Eugene
Zambuto, Frank
Zamparelli, Virginio
Zaruba, John A.
Zdeblick, William
Zeitlin, Harold Robert
Zelasko, George J.
Zichittella, Carlo John
Zielinski, Richard
Zolads, Edward J.
Zoldowski, Henry
Zoltowski, Edmund Paul
Zullo, Roland
Zurawski, Henry Albert

FOUR-YEAR SMITH-HUGHES VOCATIONAL COURSES

Bonvini, Alfred P. Jr. ....Linotype
Bratta, Sam D. ....Foundry
Byrnes, James ....Printing
DiDomenico, Renio ....Radio
Donarski, Clarence E. S...Machine
Donatiello, John Frank...Printing
Fortino, Frank Ralph.......Auto
Los, Andrew J. ....Machine
Mangalavite, Charles George.Auto
Marino, William Dennis..Printing
Markel, Gus P. ....Printing
Ploughman, Robert A...Linotype
Pudelek, Robert Harry......Auto
Rozanski, Chester ....Auto
Rutkowski, Edwin Mathew
.....................Printing
Sikora, Richard T. ......Machine
Smolucha, Stanley T. ...Machine
Stachowski, Eugene T. ..Machine
Valenti, Lawrence ......Machine

DU SABLE HIGH SCHOOL

Adams, John
Allen, Ruther Belle
Ambrose, Samuel
Armstrong, Matthew Anthony
Ayers, Evelyn M.
Bailey, James Andrew
Bailey, Natalie Delores
Banks, Essie Beatrice
Barrett, Vera Louise
Beach, Lorenzo Cornelius, Jr.
Bearden, Gloria Jean
Beasley, John B.
Bell, Mary Pearl
Bell, Zelda Delores
Bennett, James R.
Berry, George, Jr.
Blackwell, Ulysses Edward
Blair, Jerome Drew
Beatner, Guirdina Betty

Bohannon, Ruth DeLois
Bohannon, William Alonso
Boone, Marceine Ethel
Bostwick, William G.
Brackens, Myrtle Louise
Bradley, Edreana Queen
Bradley, Paris A.
Brantley, Delores Mae
Brantley, Lawrence
Bratton, Jerry
Brawer, Mildred
Brewer, Jack Jr.
Brown, Anna Mae
Brown, Emily L.
Brown, Jeanne Elnora
Brown, Lois Alicia
Browne, Lautharee DeVoronie
Buckhalter, Sarah Martha
Burns, Bertha Louise
Caillouet, Lucian
Campbell, David William
Canty, Thomas Bernard
Carson, Jacqueline
Carson, Vuelta G.
Cartman, Alfred Lawrence
Charleston, Daisy Belle
Chipchase, Julian M.
Christopher, Cleo Edna
Clay, Bertha Florence
Cokiegee, Delores Francine
Cole, Lester A.
Collins, Erlene Louise
Collins, Ernest
Connell, Briggs M., Jr.
Creed, Gerald B.
Creswell, Leonard
Cruce, Elisabeth Arnetta
Crump, Mary Irene
Culumns, Ione Yvonne
Cunningham, Sam Langford
Davis, Carolyn
Davis, Charles
Davis, Dorothy Louise
Davis, Eddie C.
Davis, John L.
Davis, Theodore
DeCuir, Earnise Talmadge
Dent, Ellen
DePriest, LaVergne W.
Dickerson, Leon R.
Dixon, Jeannine Ethel
Dixon, Margaret
Douglas, Genevieve Bernice
Driver, Alberta Edna
Dunn, Henry E.
Dunams, Berthella
Dyles, Jeannie Virdell
Edwards, David
Emmons, Dudley Atkins
Erwin, Alan
Evans, George Glenn
Evans, Rosa Lee
Fair, Jesse Jerome
Florence, Magnolia
Foster, Irene
Franklin, Frances Anita
Freeman, George Thomas
Garnett, Ruth Elziabeth
Garrett, Dorothy
Gideon, Curtisteen
Gilliam, June
Gilliam, Minnie Mae
Gilmore, Curtis Columbus
Goosby, Coetta Louvenia
Grant, Gertrude Henrietta
Grant, Roy Lewis
Gray, Doris Elizabeth
Gray, Jeanne Hortense
Greene, Josephine
Guice, Juanita Marcia
Guilford, Clara
Hall, Tevelda
Hamilton, Joyce Lee Etta
Handy, Anthony
Handy, Copeland J.
Harris, Crasious Powell

Harris, William Louis
Hart, Jimmie Lee
Harth, Ramond Earl
Hayes, Nora Ellen
Henderson, Thomasene D.
Hicks, Goria Luvenia
Hicks, James Arthur
Hill, Elizabeth Charlotte
Hines, Willa Mae
Hoffman, Yvonne Margaret
Hogan, Ouida Marie
Hooper, Fred
Hull, Frieda M.
Hunter, George Tanner
Hyde, William
Jackson, Alfred
Jackson, Chester Richard
Jackson, Frank J.
Jackson, Samuel Augustus
Jackson, Sterling K.
Jenkins, Ira Mae
Jenkins, Theodore D.
Johns, Kenneth
Johnson, Annette
Johnson, Bessie L.
Johnson, Betty Lee
Johnson, Elizabeth
Johnson, Frank
Johnson, Juanita Cassandra
Johnson, Ruby Lee
Johnson, Walter Louis
Jones, Gloria Dawn
Jones, Lavenia
Jones, Ruby F.
Jones, Samuel L.
Jordan, Irma Bernice
Joyner, Marilyn
Kaiser, Velma Adrene
Kelley, Donald Michael
Kidd, Paul Ellis
Lawrence, Delores Rosemond
Laws, Calvin
Laws, Herbert
Liddell, Anna Marie
Leinburger, Olive
Linder, Charles G.
Lindsey, Mary Frances
Little, Juanita Threase
Lockett, Marion Louise
Lovette, Harold Leroy
Lucas, Tommie Jean
Luke, Loretta Zelda
Mailey, Arleen
Mailey, Eleanora
Manning, Donald M.
Manns, Caldron
Marshall, Myrtice Ursula
Marshall, Williar Edward
Mason, Nathaniel
Matthews, James A.
Matthews, Mildred Lucile
Maxil, Louis
McCray, Frankie Mae
McDaniels, Mattie Tiena
McDowell, Marion Betty
McFall, Ola
McGhee, Eleanor
Merrida, Bernice B.
Merrill, Bernice
Meyers, Wilhelmina
Miller, Edyth Marie
Miller, Jean
Miller, Russell Orville
Mines, Floyd Ledle
Mitchell, Eugene Lawrence
Moore, Flarzell S.
Moore, Gloria Evelyn
Morse, Wilhelmina
Nance, Gertrude Bernice
Nance, Jeddie
Nellums, Danny, Jr.
Nelson, Mary Bell
Norris, Elizabeth J. Hodges
Oliver, Alfred
Outten, James Clarence
Parker, Jean Ella

Parrish, Maurice
Parrish, Walter
Patterson, Vivian
Perkins, Rosa Bele
Peterson, William George
Phillips, Helen Mae
Pierce, Maunds, Jr.,
Pointer, Ima Lou
Powell, Bettye Jean
Powell, Farrow R.
Powers, Odebell E.
Radford, Mary Margaret
Ragland, Sadie Mae
Ramsey, Marie Elizabeth
Randall, Lamar
Randolph, Irma Ruth
Ray, Alta Marie
Redd, Jerry Leen
Reed, Margaret Mary
Reed, Maxine Annie
Reese, Lloyd Noble
Rhinehart, Andrew
Rice, Edward S.
Rice, John
Roach, George
Robinson, Delores Edna
Robinson, Etta
Roper, Mamie Leora
Ross, Glenn Asey
Rowls, Margaret
Sanders, Ruby Marie
Scates, Vassie Lee
Scurlock, Helen Charlotte
Shedd, Louise
Shell, Ulysses
Slaughter, Corrine Erma
Simpson, Frieda Delores
Smith, Albert
Smith, Andrew Obidiah
Smith, Edith R.
Smith, Olen V.
Smith, Stanford S.
Sommerville, Galileo L.
Spear, John, Jr.
Stacker, Clarence
Starcks, Milford LeRoy
Stewart, Edward
Stephens, Doris Kate
Stitt, Celesta
Storey, Jeannette
Strong, John Jr.
Suthern, Frances Olivia
Taylor, Dorothy Lee
Thomas, Lewis E.
Thomas, Lewis
Thomas, William David
Thompson, Almeta Pauline
Thompson, Jacqueline
Thurman, Hubert
Tillman, Verona
Tinsley, Alberta
Towns, Elaine Mercedes
Troup, Johnny
Tucker, Ellen
Tukes, Alma
Turner, Arzella
Turner, Vivian Anita
Tyson, James A.
Tyson, Warren
Vaughn, LaVerne
Wade, Edna
Walker, Charlesetta
Walker, Elisha William
Walker, John Ivory
Walker, Rosie L. V.
Walton, Barbara Jean
Warfield, Bessie Mae
Washington, Clara Mae
Washington, Harold
Washington, Ora Lee
Waugh, Arthur Day
Wheeler, Charlene Toni
Whitehurst, Henry
Wiggan, Joyce Eneatha
Wiley, Richard M.
Williams, Carrie Lou

Figure 9. DuSable High School graduating roster (1946).

father, in 1952.[81] He worked as an attorney in private practice, as an assistant prosecutor, and as an arbitrator for the Illinois Industrial Commission (1960-1964).

Political Career

Political life for Harold had begun in his youth in the precinct of which his father was captain. Harold formally entered politics in 1954, after the death of his father in 1953. His first political office was Democratic precinct captain. He then rose through Chicago's political ranks, serving the public like his father in numerous appointed and elected capacities including assistant corporation counsel (1954-1958).

Washington served in the Illinois State Senate from 1976 to 1980, where he chaired the Committee on Public Health, Welfare and Corrections and the Legislative Reference Bureau. As an Illinois State Representative (1964-1976), he chaired the Judiciary Committee. He was a founder of the State Legislature's Black Caucus. He authored major legislation for corrections code reform, medical malpractice insurance regulation, financial aid for minority small businesses, and for recognition of the birthday of Dr. Martin Luther King, Jr. as a state holiday.

In 1977, Washington was a candidate for mayor of the City of Chicago in the special Democratic primary election following the death of Mayor Richard J. Daley. It is said that this was the only election Washington ever lost.

In November, 1980, Harold was elected to the United States Congress with a majority of more than 95% of the votes cast. He served on three committees in Congress: Education and Labor, Judiciary, and Government Operations.

Harold Washington was elected Mayor of Chicago as a reform Democrat on April 12, 1983, scoring an upset victory over old-line "machine" Democrats and a racially divisive Republican campaign. He won the 1983 election with 53.6 percent of the votes (a margin of 78,158 votes) and was reelected on April 7, 1987, with 53 percent of the votes. In both elections he won due to the collective strength of a rainbow coalition of Blacks, Whites, Hispanics, Asians, women, the elderly, the handicapped, and other groups heretofore excluded by the regular Democratic party. Out of this unique coalition and Washington's capable leadership, real reform of local government began to take shape.

---

[81] Northwestern University Law School, "Who Was Who In America," 1952, Chicago, Ill.

During the four years and seven months that he served, Mayor Harold Washington left the City of Chicago a remarkable record of leadership and accomplishment. His administration's operating theme was "Chicago Works Together" and, thanks to his leadership, that's exactly what it did. Through his intellect, sound judgment and compassion, he was able to lead Chicago to a new age when the government truly served all of its citizens, not just a select few. One of his greatest accomplishments was his investment in Chicago's neighborhoods, carrying out many of the reforms his father, Roy Washington, had dreamed of achieving. On the morning of the day he died, the Mayor was at a ground-breaking ceremony in the Kenwood/Oakland community. Through general obligation bonds and state and federal funding, Harold Washington invested more than $300 million for city-wide neighborhood street, sidewalk and sewer improvements, the largest neighborhood investment in Chicago's history.

Mayor Harold Washington collapsed at his desk in his office at City Hall on Wednesday, November 25, 1987, and was taken to Northwestern Memorial Hospital where, at 1:36 p.m., he was pronounced dead.[82] He was 65 years old. Death was attributed to a heart attack. He was buried in Oak Wood Cemetery on November 30, 1987.[83]

Genealogical Summary

Harold Lee WASHINGTON
    born 15 April 1922 at Chicago, Cook Co., IL
    married Nancy Dorothy FINCH 22 July 1942 at Chicago, Cook Co., IL
    died 25 November 1987 at Chicago, Cook Co., IL

---

[82] *Chicago Sun-Times*, "A Special Memorial Section," Tuesday, 8 December, 1987, p. 1.

[83] Ibid., p. 10.

Figure 10. Photograph of Harold Washington monument (1991).

Pedigree Chart of Harold Lee Washington

This pedigree chart illustrates graphically the direct ancestors of Harold Lee Washington, who is in the first position on the left. Direct ancestors are parents, grandparents and great-grandparents.

This is a single-line pedigree chart which includes Harold's paternal (father) line only. His maternal (mother) line of ancestors was not researched and therefore is not included in this compiled genealogy.

On this pedigree chart the father of Arbella D. Weeks (who was the grandmother of Harold Washington) is listed as Sep Hamilton, who is believed to have been her stepfather. Because she often used the surname Hamilton, he may have adopted her. Further explanation can be found in the section on Arbella Hamilton/Weeks on page 76.

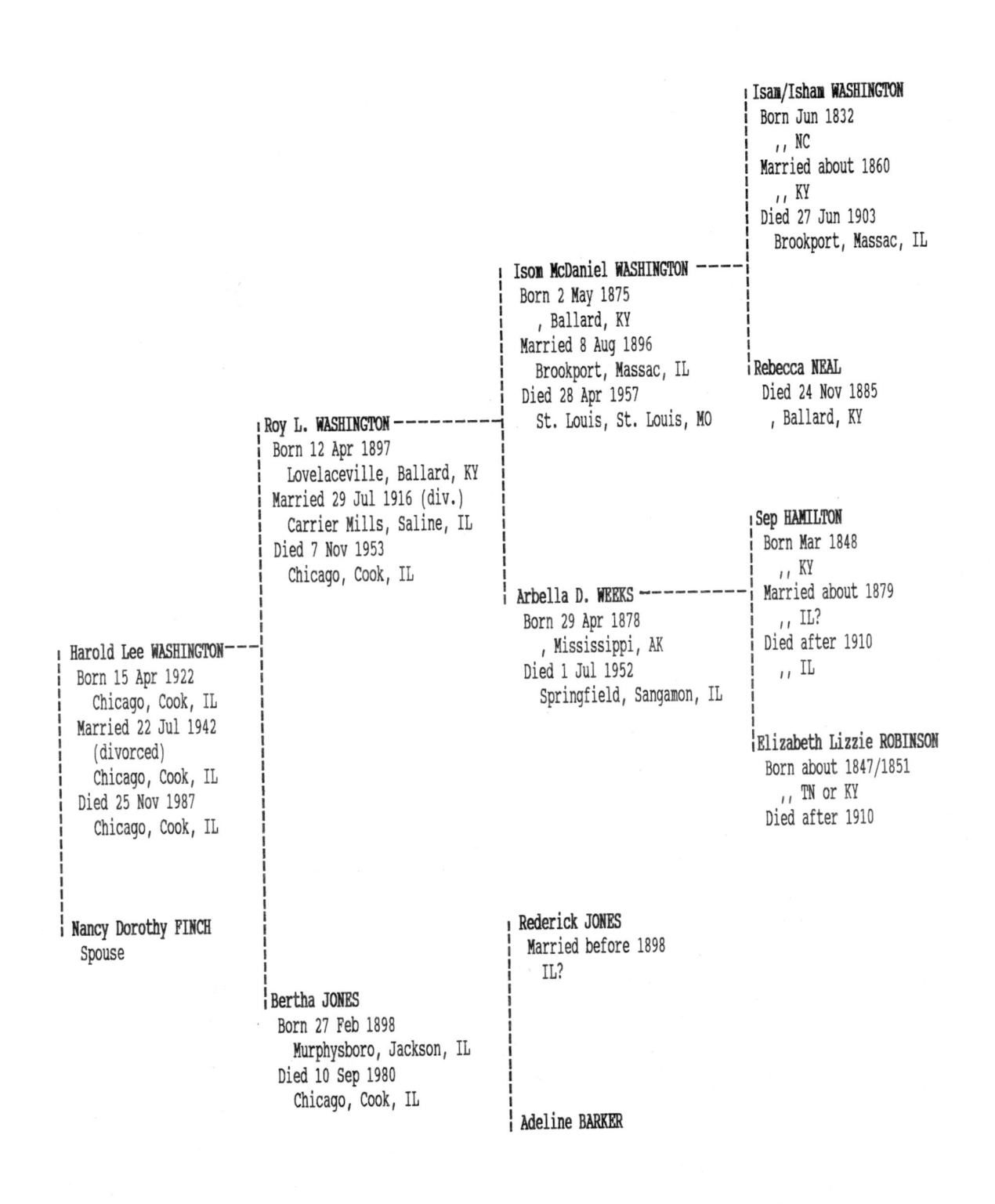

```
                                                             | Isam/Isham WASHINGTON
                                                             | Born Jun 1832
                                                             |   ,, NC
                                                             | Married about 1860
                                                             |   ,, KY
                                                             | Died 27 Jun 1903
                                                             |   Brookport, Massac, IL
                           | Isom McDaniel WASHINGTON --------|
                           | Born 2 May 1875
                           |   , Ballard, KY
                           | Married 8 Aug 1896
                           |   Brookport, Massac, IL          | Rebecca NEAL
                           | Died 28 Apr 1957                 | Died 24 Nov 1885
                           |   St. Louis, St. Louis, MO       |   , Ballard, KY
    | Roy L. WASHINGTON ----|
    | Born 12 Apr 1897
    |   Lovelaceville, Ballard, KY
    | Married 29 Jul 1916 (div.)
    |   Carrier Mills, Saline, IL                             | Sep HAMILTON
    | Died 7 Nov 1953                                         | Born Mar 1848
    |   Chicago, Cook, IL                                     |   ,, KY
                                                             | Married about 1879
                                                             |   ,, IL?
                           | Arbella D. WEEKS ----------------| Died after 1910
                           | Born 29 Apr 1878                 |   ,, IL
                           |   , Mississippi, AK
                           | Died 1 Jul 1952
                           |   Springfield, Sangamon, IL      | Elizabeth Lizzie ROBINSON
| Harold Lee WASHINGTON----|                                  | Born about 1847/1851
| Born 15 Apr 1922                                            |   ,, TN or KY
|   Chicago, Cook, IL                                         | Died after 1910
| Married 22 Jul 1942
|   (divorced)
|   Chicago, Cook, IL
| Died 25 Nov 1987
|   Chicago, Cook, IL
                                                             | Rederick JONES
                                                             | Married before 1898
                                                             |   IL?
| Nancy Dorothy FINCH
  Spouse
                           | Bertha JONES
                           | Born 27 Feb 1898
                           |   Murphysboro, Jackson, IL
                           | Died 10 Sep 1980
                           |   Chicago, Cook, IL
                                                             | Adeline BARKER
```

Figure 11. **Pedigree chart of Harold Washington.**

Part II

METHODOLOGY USED IN RESEARCH OF THE WASHINGTON FAMILY

The Ancestry of Mayor Harold Washington

Researching the ancestry of the late Mayor Harold Washington reveals, perhaps, the source of some of the characteristics of greatness which were so evident in his life. Mr. Washington's family history research is a typically difficult case study of African-American genealogical research. It is presented here for the benefit of others, of all races, who desire to trace their families' roots.

Tracing a family tree is essentially establishing through documents, certificates, and other evidence the child-to-parent relationship back through as many generations as there are reliable records to substantiate those relationships, or enough indirect evidence to establish the relationship through a preponderance of evidence.

The place to begin solving any genealogical problem is with what is known. An orderly, logical, step-by-step search from the present to the past, from the known to the unknown, keeps the research from becoming overwhelming and actually speeds it up by helping the researcher avoid branching off into interesting but collateral lines. The research of Harold Washington's family started with information readily available: printed articles which gave some of his family background, his newspaper obituaries, his death certificate. These collected bits of information started a search which would continue back to the mid-1860s. Each article and certificate was examined for important details.

At the beginning of this research, Harold's name, date and place of birth and death were known from the articles printed in Chicago newspapers and magazines. These secondary sources provided the researcher with clues and evidence. However, a genealogist never relies solely on secondary sources; he tries to go beyond that evidence to examine the primary sources — which led us to the Illinois and Cook County Vital Records.

A modern-day death certificate usually gives the deceased person's name, birth and death dates, birth and death places, marital status, the cause of death, the funeral director and the place of burial. Also included are the name and birth places of the deceased person's parents, including the mother's maiden name, if known.

The written memorial program distributed at Harold's funeral services told where he was born and educated and who his parents were. In the beginning days of research, Harold's birth and death certificates and the newspaper articles and eulogies about him were genealogical gold mines. These sources revealed the date and place of Harold's birth, his parents' names, and the misinformation that he was one of eleven children. Actually, he was the fourth and last child born to Roy and Bertha (Jones) Washington, but one of the eleven children born to Bertha. Other information on the memorial program led to research in school and military records.

Harold Washington's memorial services program provided the foundation data for the Washington genealogy research. After collecting the genealogical data and family history on Harold's life, research began on the lines of his father and mother. Harold's father, Roy L. Washington, was well known in Chicago politics. Information about him was found in his political campaign materials, city directories, and death notices. His death certificate gave his birth date, 12 April 1897, and the place as Lovelaceville, Ballard County, Kentucky. Roy's parents' names were given on his death certificate as I.A.D. Washington and Arbella Hamilton. Roy's father survived him, and his name is given in Roy's obituary as "the Rev. Isaac Washington of Springfield [Illinois]" (see Fig. 12).

Searching for Harold's Father, Roy Washington: 1900 Census

A search of the Cook County records for the marriage license of Roy L. Washington and Bertha Jones turned up no such record. Surrounding counties' records were searched, but still no clue surfaced to indicate where they were married. The known information about Roy L. and Bertha indicates that Harold's parents were divorced. Often the date of marriage is given in the divorce proceedings. A search of the Chicago vital records index for the divorce decree of Roy L. and Bertha (Jones) Washington proved to be fruitful: there was a sworn statement that they were married at Carrier Mills, Saline County, Illinois on 29 July 1916. A copy of their marriage record was obtained from the Saline County Clerk's office, Harrisburg, Illinois.

At this point, there was still no definitive evidence of who Roy's parents were. Roy's death certificate gave his parents' names as I.A.D. Washington and Arbella Hamilton. His obituary said his father's name was the Rev. Isaac Washington of Springfield, Illinois. We knew that Roy L. was born prior to the 1900 census, so searching for him in his parents' household enumeration was the next step in the Washington family research. This is a relatively quick and easy step for those who are familiar with searching the Census. The 1900 census is indexed by sound for each head of household on a state-by-state basis. A search of the Kentucky Soundex for Washingtons revealed that there were only two Washington families living in Ballard County in 1900. Isam and Mack were the heads of these families.

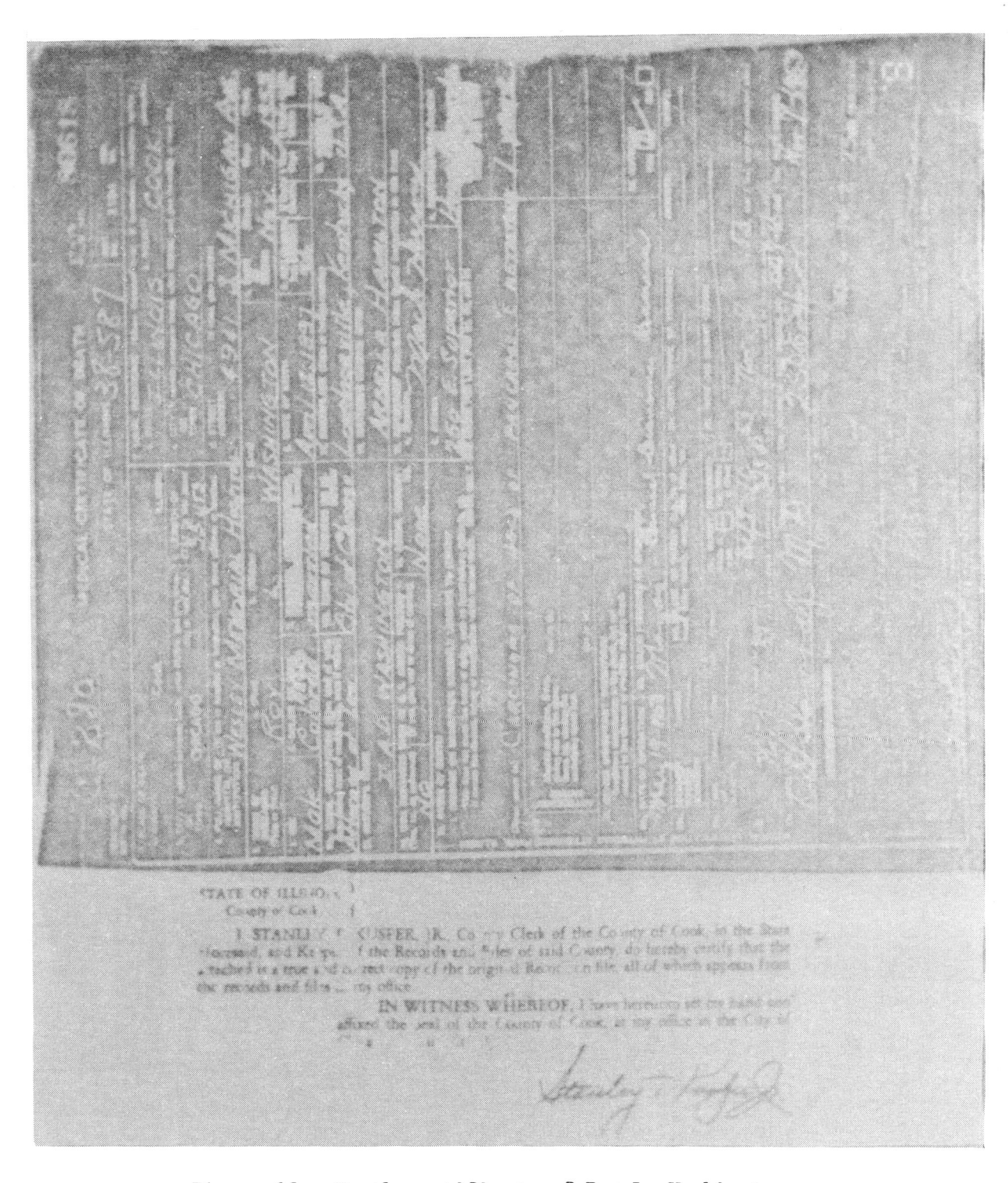

Figure 12. Death certificate of Roy L. Washington.

The 1900 census names each person and gives his or her relationship to the head of the household. The census also gives the month and year of each person's birth, his or her place of birth, the number of years a couple has been married, and for women, the number of children born to them and how many of the children are alive. The Ballard County, Kentucky census for 1900 gave direct evidence of Roy's father's name and provided much information about Roy, his father Mack, and Isam Washington, later proved to be Mack's father:

1900 CENSUS: Magisterial Dist. #2, Ballard County, KY ED 2 page 150B
Washington, Isam and wife and family living next door to:

```
                                                        1  2  3[84]
Washington, Mack head b m May 1875  25 married 4yrs     KY NC KY
   Arbella H wife     b f Apr 1880  19 married 4yrs 2-2 kids KY UN UN
   Roy son            b m Jan 1897   2 single          KY KY KY
   Lizzie dau         b f Oct 1899  9/12 single        KY KY KY
```

Searching for Harold's Grandfather, Mack Washington: 1900 Census

Examining the Census's information regarding Mack Washington revealed that he was born in May 1875, was 25 years old, and had been married four years. His wife, Arbella H. Washington, was born in April 1880, was nineteen years old, had been married four years and was the mother of two children, both of whom were then living. Mack's oldest child was Roy, born in January 1897, two years old; his other child was Lizzie, born in October 1899, age 9/12 of a year. Although there is a discrepancy of information between the 1900 census and Roy's death certificate concerning the month of his birth and his father's name, the preponderance of evidence leads us to accept these records as positive identification for Roy's parents.

The 1900 Census provided clues and supporting evidence of a father-and-son relationship between Isam Washington and Mack Washington. They were living next door to each other and it appears that Isom Mack D. was named after his father, Isam.

1900 CENSUS: BALLARD COUNTY, KY, MAGISTERIAL DISTRICT #2 ED #2 SHEET 9
188-189 WASHINGTON, ISAM HEAD-BLACK-MALE-JUNE 1832-67 YEARS-MARRIED 14
                                                   YEARS   NC NC NC[85]
```
"    MARY J. WIFE-  "  FEMALE-MAY 1850-50 YEARS-3 CHILDR.-
                                                3 ALIVE  KY KY KY
"    SCHOOLER  SON- "  MALE-DEC 1888-11 YEARS-SINGLE
                                                         KY NC KY
```

---

[84] (1) birthplace; (2) father's birthplace; (3) mother's birthplace.

[85] (1) birthplace; (2) father's birthplace; (3) mother's birthplace.

```
         WASHINGTON, ARTIMIS 6 -DAU-    "   FEMALE-MAY 1887-13 YEARS-SINGLE
                                                                  KY KY KY
              "  EZEKIEL R 6 -SON       "   MALE-OCT 1893-6 YEARS-SINGLE
                                                                  KY KY KY
```

Searching for Harold's Great-Grandfather, Isam Washington: 1900 Census

Living next door to Mack Washington's family in 1900 was the only other Washington, single or household, in the whole of Ballard County: Isam Washington, his wife and family. This household included Isam Washington, born in June 1832 in North Carolina, 67 years old and married for fourteen years. His wife was Mary J. Washington, born May 1850, 50 years old, also married fourteen years; next was listed Schooler G. Washington, Isam's son, born December 1888, eleven years old. Also living in his home were Artimis Washington, Isam's grand-daughter, born in May 1887, thirteen years old, and Ezekiel R. Washington, Isam's grandson, born in October 1893, six years old. It is not now known whose children they were, but it is suspected they were one of Isam's sons' children. Because Schooler G. was born after Isam and Mary J. were married, it can be assumed that he was not only Isam's son, but also Mary's child.

Other evidence in the Census indicating a father-and-son relationship: Mack D. said his father was born in N.C., Isam said his birth place was N.C., and Isam was the right age to be Mack D.'s father.

The census showed that Mary J. Washington was the mother of three children, all of whom were living. Schooler G., age eleven, must have been the youngest of these. Mary stated that she had been married fourteen years; Mack Washington was twenty-five at this time. This evidence indicates that Mary was not Mack's natural mother, because she was married to Isam eleven years after Mack was born. This data tells the researcher that Mary probably had two older children by a previous marriage. It is concluded that Mack was the son of an earlier wife of Isam who had died prior to about 1886, when Isam married Mary.

The researcher next wanted to locate a marriage record for Isam and Mary J. Marriage records give the maiden name of the bride and sometimes the ages of the bride and groom, information which will help the researcher further in searching for the bride's parents.

Based on census data, Isam and Mary J. were married about 1886. A search of the county vital records was made to locate the marriage record of Isam and Mary J. The Ballard County, Kentucky Colored Marriage Bonds, 1880-1905 have been indexed and microfilmed. There were five Washington marriage bonds found in these records.

Vol.-Pg.	The marriage of:	Date:
H - 95	Albert Washington and Ida Stahl	3 Jun 1885
H - 110	Isom Washington and Elizabeth Frasier	30 Dec 1885
B - 112	Sallie Washington and John Stahl	8 Mar 1886
I - 25	Ida Washington and Henry Blank	27 Feb 1893
I - 418	Avella Washington and Thomas Easley	25 Dec 1903

At this point in the research, there had not been any other Washington family, either Black or White, found living in Ballard County. Examining the five marriage bonds closely provided the researcher with strong evidence that all the Washingtons were related and most likely this was Isam's second marriage and the marriages of four of his children.

At times, genealogical research seems to be a constant stream of discrepancies. The newest one on the Washington family tree was the apparent inconsistency in the names of Isam's second wife. In the 1900 census, Isam's wife's name is given as Mary J. On the marriage bond, Isam's wife is given as Elizabeth Frasier. At first, it looked as though these were two different couples; however, there were three pieces of evidence which provided the researcher with a strong logical case for Mary J. Washington and Elizabeth Frasier being one and the same person. First, there were no other Washingtons living in the county; second, Isam and Mary J. said they had been married for fourteen years in June, 1900; and third, the Isom Washington and Elizabeth Frasier marriage on 30 December 1885 meant that in June 1900 they had been married fourteen and a half years. These clues and evidence led to this conclusion, that Isam Washington married in 1885 a widowed woman whose name was Mrs. Mary Elizabeth (Howell) Frasier.

Moving Forward: the 1910 Census

The next step in the Washington family research was to locate Isam, Isom, Mack D. and Roy L. Washington in the Ballard County, Ky. 1910 Census (censuses having been taken roughly every ten years). A search was made of Ballard and surrounding counties in Kentucky, but none of the Washingtons was found. Probate records of Ballard Co. were checked, nothing was found. Moving back to the known, Roy L. and Bertha's divorce decree indicated they had been married in Illinois. A Kentucky map showed Ballard County was located next to the Ohio River across from Illinois.

The 1910 Soundex for Illinois was checked. Mack Washington and his family were found in White county, Illinois. Because neither Isam or his wife Mary Elizabeth Howell Frasier were found in Ballard Co., Ky. 1910 Census, nor the 1910 Census of Illinois, it was assumed they had passed away.

Mack, as head of his household, was enumerated in:

1910 CENSUS, Second District River, Cairo City, White Co, IL ed 136 P 62
378-391
    Washington, Mack head m b 34 married 13yrs KY NC NC[86]
      minister
      Arbella wife f b 30 married 13yrs 4-3 kids IL NC? OH?
      Roy son m b 13 single KY KY IL
      Lizzie dau f b 10 single KY KY IL
      Booker T son m b 5 single IL KY IL

The census indicated Mack Washington to be age 34, married thirteen years, and born in Kentucky with both parents born in North Carolina. He was a minister and rented his home. His wife, Arbella, was thirty, married thirteen years, and the mother of four children, three of whom were then living. Her birthplace was listed as Illinois and her parents' birthplaces were listed as North Carolina and Ohio. Mack's children were Roy, 13, born in Kentucky; Lizzie, 10, also born in Kentucky; and Booker T., 5, born in Illinois. The Massac County, IL birth record of Booker T. indicates he was the third child, born 22 Sept. 1904. Therefore Arbella and Mack's fourth child must have been born after Booker T.

Collateral Lines: the 1880 Census

At this stage in the Washington genealogical research, we can pause and take a look at the whole Washington family tree. What information about Harold Washington's ancestry can be proved and documented? It has been documented that his father was Roy L. Washington (1897-1953); that Roy's father was Isom Mack D. Washington (1875-1957); and that Isam Mack D.'s father was Isam Washington (1832-1903). But what of the other children born to these three generations of families? What is known or can be learned about the first marriage of Isam (b. 1832) and any other children born to that marriage, i.e., the siblings of I. Mack D. Washington?

The place to start looking for the answers to these questions is again with what we already know. First, there is evidence that the Washington family was in Ballard County in 1885 (Albert's and Isom's marriages), 1900, and 1910 (U.S. censuses). The family may have been there for the 1880 census enumeration. This was the logical step for our research. Although this census is supposed to be indexed for every household with a child under the age of ten years, some families are missing from the index as well as from the census itself.

---

[86] Birthplace; father's birthplace; mother's birthplace.

When the Washington family did not appear on the 1880 census index (Soundex), a line-by-line search of the entire Ballard County, Kentucky census was conducted. Unfortunately, not one Washington was enumerated therein. Was the family missed by the census taker? Or had they moved to another county or state? Both of these suggestions are very real possibilities. The interested researcher could begin a search of the 1880 Illinois census to determine if the family had moved across the river into Illinois. If no evidence of the family is there, and the land and property records of Ballard and the surrounding counties in Kentucky yield no clues to the family's whereabouts, then the most probable answer is that the Washington family was for one reason or another missed during the 1880 enumeration.

Failure to locate an individual on a census schedule should not be taken as proof that this person was not in the county at that time. A variety of circumstances contribute to a number of people being missed in any particular census year.[87]

Names and dates are wonderful to have when researching a family tree, but the researcher wants to know more about the man Isam and his life. The researcher wanted more information about Isam Washington, information such as had been learned about Harold and Roy L. from material about their business and political careers, their speeches, etc. What did Isam do? How did he live? What records are available for research so more can be learned about him and his personality?

Researching Records

Here is the stumbling block to Black family history research: vital records (birth, marriage, and death) pertaining to Blacks after the Emancipation were not kept as diligently as they were for Whites. Often there are few "legal evidences" to document the births, marriages, and deaths of Blacks. The lack of genealogical record-keeping can be traced back to the days of slavery. Frederick Douglass, an ex-slave and noted author, stated:

> Genealogical trees do not flourish among slaves. . . . the father is literally abolished in slave law and slave practice. I never met with a slave who could tell me how old he was. . . . Few slave mothers knew anything of the months of the year, nor of the days of the months. They kept no family records, with marriage,

---

[87] David H. Streets, *Slave genealogy: A research guide with case studies* (Bowie, MD: Heritage Books, 1986), p. 10.

birth and death. They measure the age of their children by springtime, winter time, harvest time, planting time . . . but these soon become indistinguishable and forgotten.[88]

The scarcity of records on Blacks immediately following emancipation can probably be explained by a variety of circumstances:

. . . slaves were not considered citizens of the United States, they were forbidden to read and write, enter any legal transaction, not even a marriage contract. With no legal status of their own, there are virtually no records concerning slaves which were initiated or recorded by slaves themselves.[89]

These are just a few of the reasons Blacks probably didn't feel the same need to register their family marriages, births, and deaths as Whites did. Also, many states did not start keeping vital records until the beginning of this century. As a result, most of these records were not registered for them during and right after emancipation, which presents a stumbling block for Black family history research.

Probate Records

Probate records involve the transfer of one's property after one's death. Usually the date and place of death are listed as well as the names of heirs. A search for Isam Washington's will or administration papers in Ballard County, KY was conducted—nothing was found. Newspapers, land records, court and vital records were searched for mention of him. No record searched mentioned his death, and he was not located on the 1910 Ballard County Census. It was supposed, from this evidence, coupled with the knowledge of his advanced age, that Isam died after June 1900 and before the decade was over.

Ballard County Land and Tax Records

Land and tax records are not always available, but when they are they are most helpful and should always be searched. Tax records give a good idea of when a young man turned 21, and his economic condition. Kentucky kept yearly tax lists for all their citizens. These lists were housed in each county archive. After the Civil War most Kentucky counties kept separate lists for Blacks and Whites. David Streets, author of *Slave Genealogy*, said "Post Civil War tax lists were often the first records to

---

[88] Frederick Douglass, *My bondage and my freedom* (Urbana and Chicago: University of Illinois Press, 1987), p. 28.

[89] Ibid., David H. Streets, p. 5.

name former slaves and provide the Black family historian with valuable information about his ancestors."[90]

In the Ballard county, Kentucky, tax records, the researcher finally found Isham Washington and learned how many acres of land Isham owned and its value, on which water course they lay, the numbers and value of animals and amounts of crops grown and harvested the previous year, and the name of his nearest neighbor. The record also showed how many children were dependent upon him for support. A close study of his tax records year by year showed that his crops and animals increased.

Isham's neighbor, Woodson Fraser [sic] apparently died in 1885, after the tax record was given, and Woodson's widow and Isam/Isham were married by the 1886 tax accounting. Later on in the research, specifically in the pension papers, there were Woodson's death date, Isam/Isham's first wife's death date, and the marriage date of Elizabeth Frasier (Woodson's widow) and Isam/Isham.

A search of the 1863-1872 tax records revealed for the first time Washingtons other than Isam and his family living in Ballard Co., KY. There were four entries pertaining to the surname Washington before 1870. In the first entry, dated 1866, Isam was listed "I. Washington (colored) free Negro." No other tally there was recorded, but in 1867 there was Jef Washington, and in 1868, Isam and Dan. In 1869 there were entries for Dan, Isam and Daniel. They were listed as "(colored) free Negroes ages 21 and above." These tax records are the only known records before 1870 in which Washingtons can be found. In 1870 there were no Washingtons listed in the tax records in Ballard Co. KY, and only one seventeen-year-old male named Frank, born in Mississippi, was listed in the Census. Jef, Dan, Daniel or Frank didn't appear in any more records searched in Ballard Co.

From 1866 to 1886, Isam is listed in the twelve existing yearly tax books. From these interesting polls it was learned that Isam probably had at least seven children (see Table 1), that he mortgaged his tobacco crop each year — it is presumed to pay for the seed or other materials necessary to produce the crop — and that he grew other crops as well. Yearly, his acres, animals, crops and children increased in numbers.

If Isam did have six or more children besides Mack, where can the researcher look to find documentation of their relationship to Isam? Records show that there were four Washington marriages in Ballard County between 1885 and 1903. One name in particular rings a bell: Sallie Stahl. In what document had the name Sallie Stahl appeared? A review of records for I. Mack D. Washington revealed that he was survived by a sister,

---

[90] Ibid., p. 31.

Table 1

Tax Record of Isam/Isham Washington
Ballard Co., KY Tax Lists

1873

Isham Washington 55 Acres in Ballard Co. on Humphries Water Course: 1 male over 21; 1 hog; 2 mules; 3000 lbs. tobacco; 150 bushel corn.

1874

Isam Washington 55 Acres Ballard Co. — nearest resident, D.T. Lee; No. of Election Precinct in which situated, 4; value of land, $400: 3 cattle; value of gold, silver 7 other metalic watches and clocks, gold and silver plates and pianos - $5; total value at $0.45 per $100 = $530; 1 male over 21 years of age; 1 legal voter; 5 children between 6 and 20 years old; 9 hogs; 2500 lbs. tobacco; 125 bushels corn; 35 bushels wheat.

1875

Isham Washington 55 Acres Ballard Co. — nearest resident, D.T. Lee; No. of Election Precinct in which situated, 2; value of land, $400: 1 horse, value $20; 2 mules, value $100; 3 cattle, total value at $0.45 per $100 = $560; 1 male over 21 years of age; 1 legal voter; 1 enrolled militia; 6 children between 6 and 20 years of age; 1 hog; 3400 lbs. tobacco; 2 tons hay; 200 bushels corn; 137 bushels wheat.

1876

Isham Washington 55 Acres Ballard Co. — nearest resident, D.T. Lee; value of land, $385; 1 horse, value $40; 2 mules, value $100; 1 male over 21 years of age; 1 legal voter; 7 children between 6 and 20 years of age; 5000 lbs. tobacco; 500 bushels corn; 116 bushels wheat

1877

Isham Washington — No. of election precinct in which situated, 2; 1 horse, value $20; 2 mules, value $150 (total value $170); 1 male over 21 years of age; 1 legal voter; 5 children between 6 and 20 years old; 1 hog; 1 sheep killed by dogs, exempt $2; 5,000 lbs. tobacco; 500 bushels corn; 50 bushels wheat.

(**Table 1**, continued)
1878

    Isham Washington — No. of election precinct in which situated, 2; 2 horses, value $45; 1 mule, value $40; 3 cattle; value of pleasure carriages, barouches, buggies, stage coaches, gigs, omnibuses & other vehicles for passengers, $15; total value at $.40 per $100 = $100; 1 male over 21 years of age; 1 legal voter; 5 children between 6 and 20; 2 hogs; 2000 bushels tobacco; 500 bushels corn; 100 bushels wheat.

1879

    Isam Washington 62 Acres Ballard Co. — nearest resident, Tom Gibson; value of land, $300; 2 horses, value $40; 1 mule, value $40; 10 carriages; 10 hogs; 600 lbs. of tobacco; 350 bushels corn; 100 bushels wheat.

1880

    Isham Washington — nearest resident, Tom Gibson; 4 horses & mules, value $125; 7 children between 6 and 20; 1 hog; 9000 lbs. tobacco; 500 bushels corn; 130 bushels wheat

1884

    Isam Washington — No. of election precinct in which situted, 2; 2 horses, value $50; 1 mule, value $20; 11 hogs, value $15; 2 cattle; total value at $.47 1/2 per $100 = $85; 1 male over 21 years; 1 legal voter; 6 children between 6 and 20 years old; 1 hog.

1885

	Males over 21	Legal voters	Children (6-20)
Robert Reeves	1	1	2
Isham Washington	1	1	5
Woodson Fraser	1	1	2
Fannie Fraser	-	-	2

1886

Fany Fraser	-	-	2
Robert Reeves	1	1	2
Albert Washington	1	1	-
Isam Washington	1	1	7

No Woodson listed

Sallie Stahl of Paducah, Kentucky. This provides the evidence to prove the relationship of Sallie Washington as a child of Isam Washington.

What other evidence, either direct or indirect, could there be to establish the names of Isam's other sons and daughters? The land and property records of Ballard County again provided some clues. There were at least sixteen Washington entries in the Ballard County, KY Mortgage Books from 1880 to 1895. By studying the mortgage books, it revealed the amounts of money Isam had to borrow and the number of acres of tobacco or corn crop he was to pay for the money borrowed. Three mortgages gave us further information about the family. On 29 October 1884, Isham Washington and his son, John Ray Washington, were grantors (see Table 2). On 6 October 1886, J. Albert Washington signed a mortgage for $60.00 (see Table 3). Twice William P. Washington signed mortgages (see Table 4). These three men were probably all sons of Isam. The clues from the five Ballard County marriages can be coupled with the information learned from the tax polls and mortgage books and the 1900 census to put together a probable family of seven or more children of Isam Washington.

But what of the man? What sources can be searched to learn more about Isham Washington's life prior to 1866? Was he a slave? In the 1866 tax records of Ballard County, he is listed as a free negro man over 21 years of age. It was learned from Ballard Co. history that the Courthouse burned in 1880 and most of the county records were destroyed by fire. If Isham was freed before 1860, he should appear in the 1860 Census. This source was searched, but no Isham/Isam — or any other Washington, Black or White — was found.

Looking back at the 1900 Census, Isham/Isam said he was born (in North Carolina) in 1832. He would have been of prime military service age to have served in the Civil War. If he was in Ballard Co. Ky. during the Civil War, then it was possible that he encountered the Union forces when ex-slaves were being recruited into the regiments of the United States Colored Troops. If this is the case, then his military and pension records might answer some very important questions about his former life. A search of Kentucky military records was conducted checking the index of the military affairs department in the archives of the Kentucky Historical Society. This search proved fruitful: he was found listed as Isham Washington on the Muster Roll of Company "L", Eighth United States Colored Artillery (Heavy).

The next step in the Washington family's genealogy research was to obtain from the National Archives in Washington, D.C., copies of Isham's military and pension records to see what they reveal about his life.

Military Records of Isham Washington

It was learned from Isham's military record that he had been born in North Carolina and enlisted at the age of 40, 23 December 1864, at

Paducah, KY. His occupation was recorded as "Laborer" and he was enlisted by Captain J.H. Morgan for a period of three years. His eyes, hair and complexion were recorded as Black and his height was five feet 9 1/2". He was mustered in 23 December 1864 as a substitute (Colored) in lieu of J.S. Petree, a drafted man of Ballard County, Kentucky. (See Figure 13.)

At this point one wondered who was John Petree and why was Isham his substitute? In checking the 1870 Ballard County Census, it was found that John S. Petree (the name looked like Peters on the census but it was the correct person, the only Petree in Ballard County, 1864-1872 tax list) was a doctor with a family who owned 150-160 acres on Shawnee Creek — one time given as Humphrey's Creek (where Isham's land was located). So they must have lived near each other. It was supposed that he might have paid Isham off with land for serving for him, but his acreage remained the same. There was also speculation perhaps he could have owned Isham earlier, or his family may have owned him, but the researcher didn't pursue this search any further.

Isham Washington was discharged from the military service on 10 February 1866 at Victoria, Texas.

Pension Records of Isham/Isam and Elizabeth Washington

The pension files produce a wealth of new genealogical information concerning Isham/Isam Washington and his family. The researcher learned from his pension application papers that he had five children living when he applied for his Civil War pension. As is often the case in pension files, a list of the surviving children's names and dates of birth were given. Also, his wife's maiden name and their date of marriage were given. As is typical, either a marriage certificate or the page ripped out of the family Bible giving the date of the marriage was in the packet. In addition to showing when and where he served, his pension record gives a physical description and a record of his promotions. Other papers of interest filed in a pension packet include affidavits from friends or relatives. These bring more of the human side to one's ancestors and give us colorful insights into their lives and surroundings. There are several of these affidavits in Isam/Isham's pension files in which his neighbors testify about death dates and places, and their friendship with him and the Frasiers.

Military and pension records of Isham/Isam agree on enlistment date, place, physical description, age, place of birth and date and place of discharge. His age is listed as 40 in both records, which would place his birth around 1824. This year is off from what is listed in the 1900 Census, when he gave his age as 67. He married Rebecca Neal about March or April, 1866, calculated from the reported first child's birth.

Table 2

Tax records of Isam/Isham Washington
Ballard Co. KY Mortgage Books
Roll #977108 (1880-1902)

Ballard Co., KY Mortgage Book A Page 35: JOHN KIMMEL of Ballard Co. indebted to ISAM WASHINGTON in the sum of THIRTY DOLLARS due 1 Oct 1880, secured by: one light mouse colored horse male blind in one eye, about 14 hands high, known as the George Hutcherson mule, also about 4 acres of wheat now growing on my place, all of said property is in Ballard Co., KY. Witness my hand 7th April 1880.
JOHN KIMMEL

Recorded 11 May 1880

Ballard Co., Ky Mortgage Book B Page 109: 1 July 1881: ISAM WASHINGTON of Ballard Co., indebted to TREWALLA & BRO in the sum of TWO HUNDRED AND FIFTY DOLLARS, due Nov 1881, secured by: [either three or nine] acres of tobacco now growing on the lease taken on the land of the Widow Lovelace joining John Smiths farm. Witness my hand 1 July 1881.
ISAM WASHINGTON

Recorded 13 July 1881

Ballard Co., KY Mortgage Book B Page 112: 6 July 1881: [Robert Reeves], indebted to TREWALLA & BRO, THIRTY FOUR DOLLARS and to BUGG SMITH in the sum of TEN DOLLARS and to ISHAM WASHINGTON in the sum of FIFTY TWO & 50/100 dollars, secured by: MY PRESENT GROWING CROP OF TOBACCO AMOUNTING TO ABOUT FOUR ACRES, NOW GROWING ON THE FARM ON WHICH I NOW LIVE LYING ON THE ROAD FROM BLANDVILLE TO PADUCAH, payable 1 Nov 1881, given under my hand this July 6th 1881.

                    HIS
ROBERT   X   REEVES
                    MARK

Recorded 14 July 1881

Ballard Co., KY Mortgage Book Z Page 26: 28 Aug 1882: ISHAM WASHINGTON, indebted [to] TREWALLA BROTHERS of Hinkleville in the sum of ONE HUNDRED AND FIFTY DOLLARS, secured by: ONE CROP OF TOBACCO NOW GROWING ON MY FARM [*farm* is lined out] PLACE WHICH I LEASED FROM THE WIDOW LOVELACE FARM ADJOINING JOHN SMITHS AND JOHN PRESTONS PLACES IN BALLARD CO., KY. THE SAID CROP OF TOBACCO COVERS EIGHT ACRES OF GROUND, payable 1 Apr 1883. Witness my hand this 28th Aug 1882.
ISHAM WASHINGTON

(**Table 2**, continued)

Ballard Co., KY Mortgage Book D Page 228: 1 Sept 1884: ISHAM WASHINGTON, indebted to TREWALLA & BRO, in the sum of TWO HUNDRED AND FIFTY DOLLARS, payable 25 Jan 1885, secured by: FIVE ACRES OF TOBACCO growing on George Lovelace farm known as the Widow Lovelace farm joining Dock Frasier & John Preston. Witness my hand 1 Sep 1884.

            ISHAM WASHINGTON

Ballard Co., KY Mortgage Book D Page 261: 24 Oct 1884: ISHAM WASHINGTON & SON J.R., indebted to TREWALLA & BRO., in the sum of ONE HUNDRED DOLLARS, due 24 Oct 1884 [sic—it should be 1 Mar 1885], secured by: MY ENTIRE CROP OF TOBACCO SUPPOSED TO BE ABOUT THREE THOUSAND LBS GROWN ON THE WIDOW LOVELACE FARM IN THE YEAR 1884, delivered by 1 March 1885. Witness 24 Oct 1884.

         HIS
      ISHAM X WASHINGTON
         MARK
          HIS
     JOHN RAY X WASHINGTON
         MARK

Ballard Co., KY Mortgage Book E Page 91: 12 Sep 1885: ISHAM WASHINGTON, indebted to TREWALLA & BRO, in the sum of TWO HUNDRED AND FIFTY DOLLARS, payable on 1 Jan 1886, secured by: MY ENTIRE CROP OF TOBACCO SUPPOSED TO BE EIGHT ACRES, GROWN ON THE FARM OF ROBT. REEVES COL [colored?] KNOWN AS THE WIDOW LOVELACE FARM. Witness 12 Sep 1885.

            ISHAM WASHINGTON

Ballard Co., KY Mortgage Book E Page 421: 5 July 1886: ISAM WASHINGTON, indebted to TREWALLA BROS, in the sum of THREE HUNDRED DOLLARS, payable on 5 July 1886, secured by: MY ENTIRE CROP OF TOBACCO SUPPOSED TO BE 13 ACRES OF WHICH JOHN HOPKINS IS TO HAVE ONE FOURTH, ONE BUGGY WITH TWO SEATS AND THREE SPRINGS. Witness this day 5 July 1886

            ISHAM WASHINGTON

 Recorded 31 July 1886

Ballard County Mortgage Book E Page 552: 2 November 1886: ISAM WASHINGTON indebted to TREWALLA BROS., in the sum of THIRTY SIX DOLLARS, payable on 1 March 1887, secured by: THE REMAINING FOURTH OF MY CROP OF TOBACCO IT BEING THE ENTIRE INTEREST OF JOHN HOPKINS IN THE CROP. Witness 2 Nov 1886

            ISHAM WASHINGTON

 Recorded 10 Nov 1886

(Table 2, continued)
Ballard County, KY Mortgage Book 6 Page 48: 4 August 1887: ISAM WASHINGTON, indebted to TREWALLA BROS., in the sum of TWO HUNDRED DOLLARS, payable 1 March 1888, secured by: MY ENTIRE CROP OF TOBACCO NOW GROWING ON THE WIDOW RICH FARM IN BALLARD CO. SUPPOSED TO BE SIX ACRES, delivered by the first of March 1888. ALSO ONE SPRING BUGGY. Witness 4 Aug 1887.
I WASHINGTON

Ballard County, KY Mortgage Book I Page 91: 1 Aug 1891, ISam [sic] WASHINGTON, indebted to A G HUTCHERSON in the sum of NINETY SIX DOLLARS payable 1 NOV 1891 secured by: ONE HALF INTEREST IN MY GROWING CROP OF TOBACCO BEING ABOUT 6 ACRES ALSO ONE HALF INTEREST IN MY GROWING CROP OF CORN OF ABOUT 20 ACRES. THE GROWING CROP BEING ON THE FARM KNOWN AS THE HANON LOVELACE FARM. Witness 1 Aug 1891.
I WASHINGTON

Ballard County, KY Mortgage Book K Page 121: 28 Jan 1895, I WASHINGTON, indebted to B. FRANK BILLINGTON, in the sum of SEVENTY THREE & 10/100 DOLLARS, payable on 1 August 1895, secured by: MY ENTIRE CROP OF TOBACCO CONSISTING OF FIVE THOUSAND POUNDS AFTER DEDUCTING FROM SAID CROP OF TOBACCO A SUFFICIENT AMOUNT TO PAY THE RENT NOW DUE FOR THE YEAR 1894 ON WHICH I NOW LIVE THE AMOUNT BEING SIXTY TWO AND 50/100 DOLLARS. Witness 28 Jany 1895.
ISHAM WASHINGTON

Ballard County, KY Mortgage Book I Page 249: 9 Sep 1895: ISM [sic] WASHINGTON, indebted to B. FRANK BILLINGTON, in the sum of THIRTY DOLLARS, payable on 1 JUNE 1896, secured by: ONE & ONE HALF ACRE OF TOBACCO IT BEING M-BURG [sic] HALF OF JNO. RUSS CROP GROWING ON MY PLACE. Witness 9 Sep 1895.
I WASHINGTON

Table 3

Mortgage records of Isam/Isham Washington

Ballard County, KY Mortgage Book E Page 514: 9 Oct 1886: ALBERT WASHINGTON, indebted to TREWALLA & BROS, in the sum of SIXTY DOLLARS, payable 1 March 1887, secured by: MY ENTIRE CROP OF TOBACCO SUPPOSED TO BE TWO ACRES RAISED AND HOUSED ON THE FARM OF JS PRESTON IN BALLARD CO., KY IN THE YEAR 1886. Witness 9 Oct 1886.

JA WASHINGTON

Table 4

Mortgage records of W.P. Washington

Ballard Co., Ky. Mortgage Book F, Page 315:
This indenture made and entered into by and between William Washington and John S. Preston both of Ballard County Ky Witnesseth that for and in consideration of Seventy-five dollars this day loaned by said Preston to said Washington evidenced by his promissory note for said sum bearing even date herewith and due nine months after date. To assure the payment of said note the said Washington has this day sold unto said Preston all his present growing crop of tobacco and corn on the place of said Preston in Ballard County Ky to have and to hold same unto said Preston his heirs and assigns forever. The condition of this sale is such that should said Washington pay said note at maturity then it is to be null and void. Otherwise to remain in full force. Witness my signature this Aug 20th 1888.
                                                W P Washington

Ballard Co., Ky. Mortgage Book F, Page 89 Top:
Know all men by these presents that I.W.P. Washington of the County of Ballard and state of Kentucky have this day become Indebted to B.F. Billington in the sum of twenty-five Dollars evidenced by my promissory note of even date herewith due and payable the 25 day of Decr 1887. Now in order to better secure the payment of said note at maturity I hereby grant bargain and sell and by these presents convey unto the said B.F. Billington the following described property to wit One fourth interest in 18 acres of Corn and one fourth Interest in 7 acres of tobacco said corn and Tobacco being now cultivated on the farm formerly owned by John Swafford to have and to hold said property to said Billington his heirs and asigns forever The Conditions of the above sale are such should I or any one for . . . 23d day of Aug 1888 acknowledged before my deputy F.J. Neely be the said Reeves to be his Act and deed all of which appears from the following Endorsement to wit Acknowledged in full Aug 23 1888 Ben Flint CBCC by F J Neely DC and said Mortgage was on the 28 day of Aug 1888 lodged in my office for record and the same with said endorsement and this certificate has been duly recorded in my office. Witness my hand this the 28 day of August 1888.
                                                Ben Flint CBCC
                                                by W Y Husband DC

2 | 8 H. Art'y. |U.S.C.T.|	2 | 8 H. Art'y. |U.S.C.T.|
Isham Washington	Isham Washington
............, Co. L., 8 Reg't U.S. Col'd H. Art'y.	Corpl., Co. L., 8 Reg't U.S. Col'd H. Art'y.
Appears on **Company Descriptive Book** of the organization named above. **DESCRIPTION.**	Appears on Co. Muster-out Roll, dated Victoria, Texas Feby 10, 1866.
Age 40 years; height 5 feet 9 1/2 inches.	Muster-out to date Feby 10, 1866.
Complexion Blk	Last paid to Aug 31, 1865.
Eyes Blk; hair Blk	Clothing account:
Where born N. Carolina	Last settled ...., 186 ; drawn since $........100
Occupation Laborer	Due soldier $ 33 05/100; due U.S. $........100
ENLISTMENT.	Am't for cloth'g in kind or money adv'd $........100
When Dec 23, 1864	Due U.S. for arms, equipments, &c., $........100
Where Paducah, Ky.	Bounty paid $........100; due $........100
By whom Capt. Morgan; term 3 y'rs.	Remarks Entered service as Substitute for John S. Peters 1st Dist. Ky. Mustered for duty Dec 23, 1864. Promoted Corpl. Feby 10, 1865. Due U.S. on error on time in August Pay Rolls $33.80
Remarks: Promoted Sergt to rank from Feb. 10th 1865. Reduced to the ranks March 30th 1865.* Promoted Corpl to rank from Feby 10th 1865 Substitute for J.S. Peters 1st Dist. Ky. * Cancelled by lines	Book mark:
........, Keefer	J. L. Norris

Figure 13. Civil War military records of Isham Washington.

CEREMONY

MARRIAGE LICENSE

The Commonwealth of Kentucky.

To any Minister of the Gospel, or other person legally authorized to solemnize Matrimony:

You are permitted to solemnize the Rites of Matrimony between _I. Washington_ AND _Elizabeth Frasier_ the requirements of the law having been complied with.

Witness my signature as Clerk of _Ballard_ County Court, this _28_ day of _Dec_ _1885_

Ben Flint — Clerk.

——— Deputy Clerk.

✱ Marriage Certificate ✱

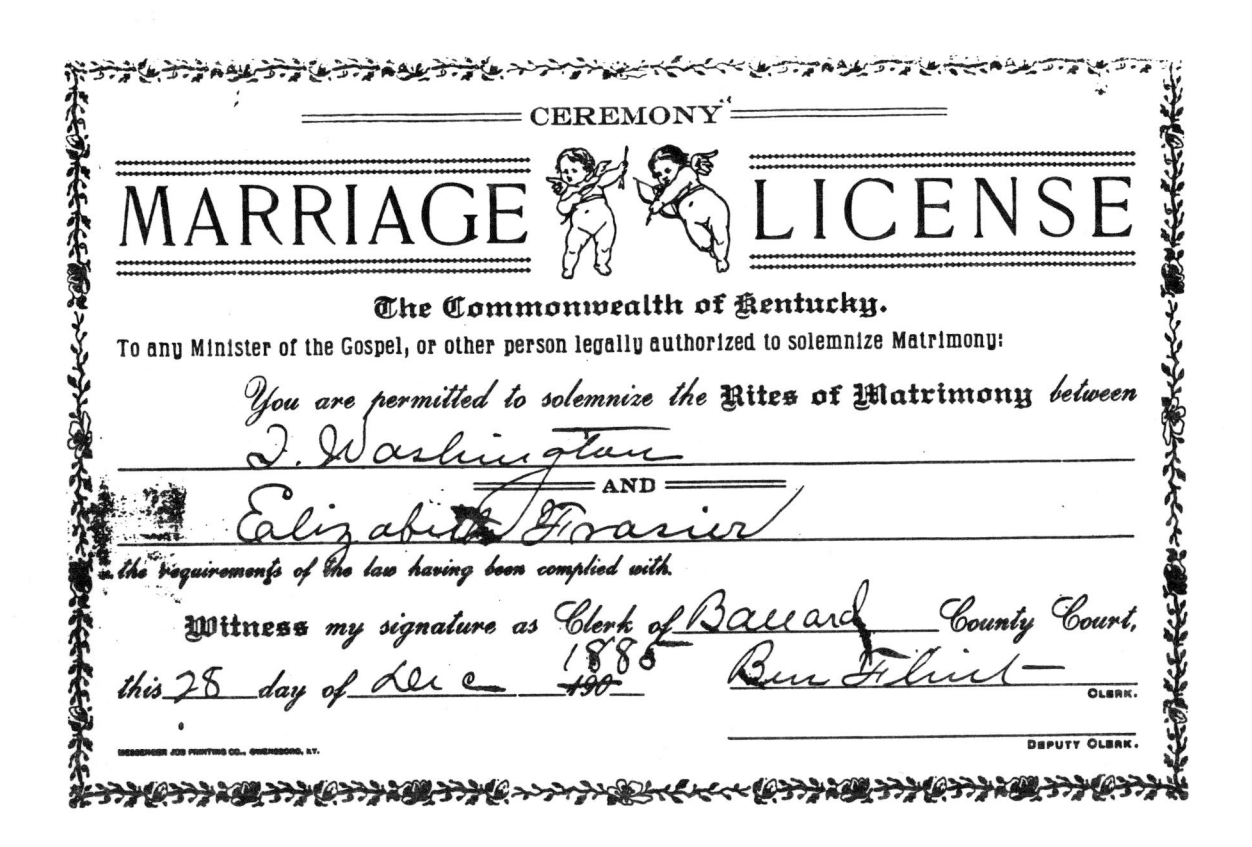

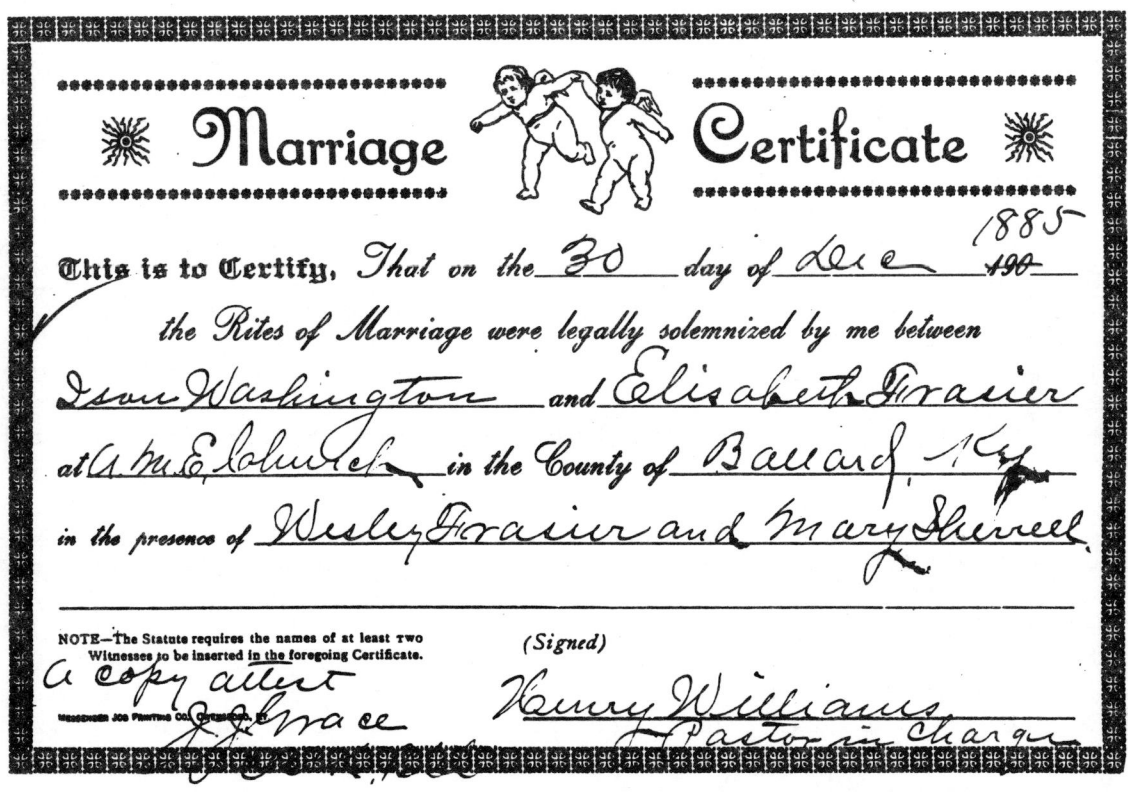

This is to Certify, That on the _30_ day of _Dec_ _1885_ the Rites of Marriage were legally solemnized by me between _Isom Washington_ and _Elisabeth Frasier_ at _A.M.E. Church_ in the County of _Ballard, Ky_ in the presence of _Wesley Frasier_ and _Mary Sherrell_

NOTE—The Statute requires the names of at least TWO Witnesses to be inserted in the foregoing Certificate.

A copy attest
J.J. Wace

(Signed)
Henry Williams,
Pastor in Charge

Figure 14. Marriage license of Isam Washington and Mary Elizabeth (Howell) Frasier.

Isham/Isam and Rebecca Neal Washington were the parents of the following children according to a document dated 7 October 1897:

```
WILLIAM PLEASANT    WAS BORNED JAY 12 1867 [sic]
SALVANY             WAS BORNED JANY 22 1869
MARY JANE           WAS BORNED AUG 2 1871
HORRANCE LEE        WAS BORNED FEBY 17 1873
ISOM McDANIEL                  MAY 2 1875
```

The same document shows that Rebecca Neal Washington died 24 Nov 1885 in Ballard Co., Ky., 4 miles N.W. of Lovelaceville, Ky.

Isham/Isam's second marriage was to Mary Jane Elizabeth (Howell) Frasier, 30 December 1885. (See Figure 14.) Mary preferred to be called Elizabeth, as in all her records she gave her name Elizabeth rather than Mary.

Isham/Isam Washington's postwar residences were in Ballard County, Kentucky until after June, 1900. Because his whereabouts after 1900 were unknown, and no evidence showed that he had left the county, it had been assumed that he died there before 1910. Now his pension records established his movements after 1900: sometime before 1903, Isham and his wife Mary Elizabeth migrated to Massac Co., Illinois, and evidence shows that he died there 27 July 1903. (See Figure 15.) His wife Elizabeth received her widow's pension after his death. She received her last pension check of $12.00 on 4 January 1913. (See Figure 16.) Isham/Isam's pension file provides the researcher with direct evidence of father-to-children relationship. He named William P., Salvany (the spelling of Salvany in this document could be a phonic variation of Sallie, or Sallie could be short for Salvany), Mary Jane, Horace Lee, and Isom McDaniel as his living children. (See Figure 17.) There is evidence in Ballard Co. tax records that he was the father of at least seven or more children. The 1870 and 1880 Censuses could have provided a direct source of who his children were, but unfortunately the whole family was missed in both census years. There was also supporting evidence in his files that Mary J., found in the 1900 Census as Isham's second wife was the same Elizabeth Frasier that he married in 1885, Mary Jane Elizabeth (Howell) Washington.

Pension papers are very helpful and they should never be overlooked. Isham/Isam's files also provided the researcher with clues in other areas to search for Isam's children. In the 1910 Census there were no Washingtons found living in Ballard Co., Ky. Isam Mack was found in White Co. Illinois in 1910, and there were no other Washingtons living there. His third child, Booker T.'s death record indicates he was born in Massac Co., Illinois in 1904. Isham Washington died in Massac Co. in 1903, and his wife died there in 1913. With these clues a search was conducted in Massac Co., Illinois for William P., Mary Jane, and Horace Lee, named as children of Isham/Isam Washington in his pension files.

Act June 27, 1890.

PENSIONER DROPPED

B. N.O. 788.076 O.K.

United States Pension Agency,

Louisville, Ky.

Aug. 6, 1903

Certificate No. 834,725

Class Invalid

Pensioner Isom Washington

Soldier

Service Corp'l L, 8" U.S.C.V.H.a.

The Commissioner of Pensions.

SIR: I have the honor to report that the above-named pensioner who was last paid at $12# to 4 May, 1903, has been dropped because of death, June 27", 1903.

Very respectfully,

D. R. Collier
United States Pension Agent.

NOTE.— Every name dropped to be thus reported at once, and when cause of dropping is death, state date of death when known.

o-9

Figure 15. Isam Washington dropped from pension roster.

69

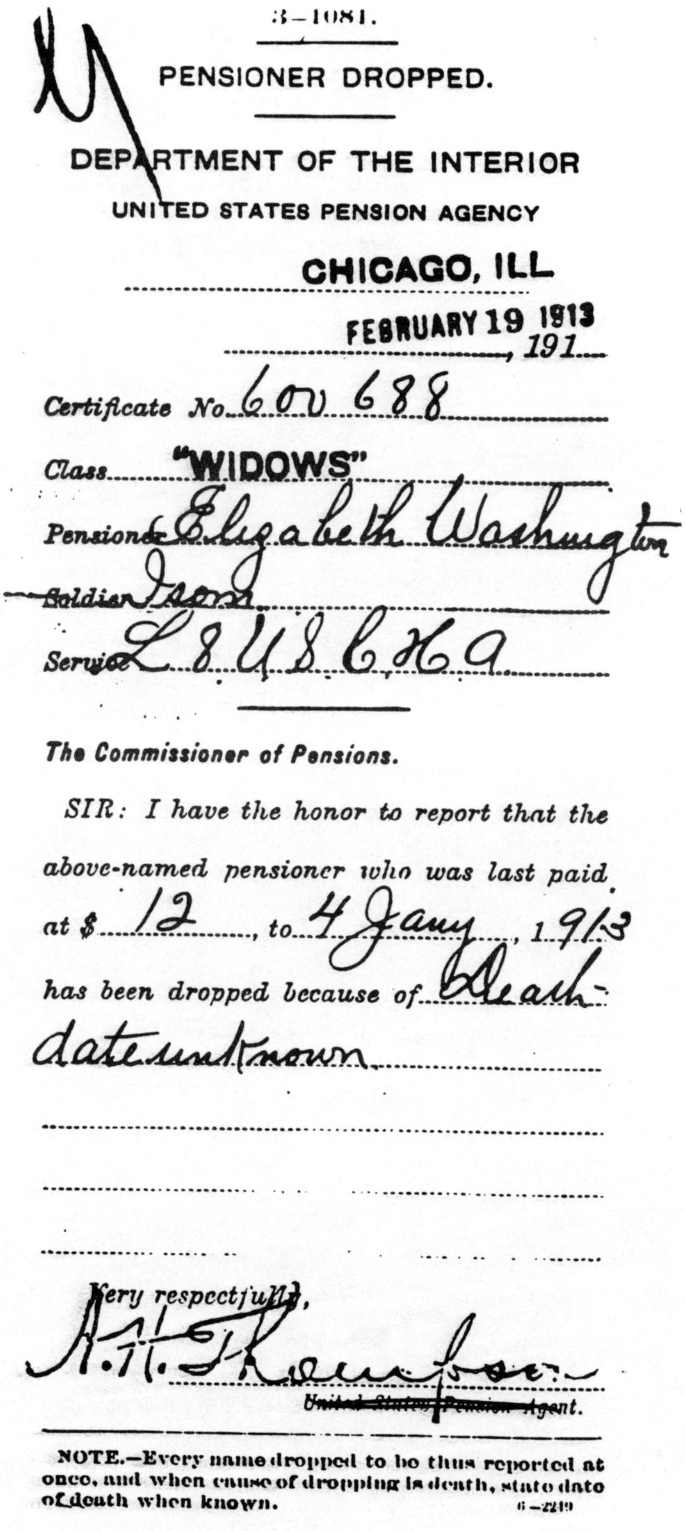

3-1081.

PENSIONER DROPPED.

DEPARTMENT OF THE INTERIOR

UNITED STATES PENSION AGENCY

CHICAGO, ILL

FEBRUARY 19 1913, 191___

Certificate No. 600 688

Class "WIDOWS"

Pensioner Elizabeth Washington

~~Soldier~~ Isom

Service 28 U S C H a

The Commissioner of Pensions.

SIR: I have the honor to report that the above-named pensioner who was last paid at $ 12, to 4 Jany, 1913 has been dropped because of death date unknown

Very respectfully,

A. H. Thompson
~~United States Pension~~ Agent.

NOTE.—Every name dropped to be thus reported at once, and when cause of dropping is death, state date of death when known. 6-2219

Figure 16. Mary Elizabeth Washington dropped from pension roster.

Southern Div. 3–173. Ex'r.

No. 831-751
Isom H. Washington
Co. L. 8 Reg't U.S.C. Vol. H.A.

Department of the Interior,
BUREAU OF PENSIONS.

Washington, D. C., October 11, 1897

Sir:

Will you kindly answer, at your earliest convenience, the questions enumerated below? The information is requested for future use, and it may be of great value to your family.

Very respectfully,

I. Washington
Lovelaceville
Ky

H. Clay Evans
Commissioner

No. 1. Are you a married man? If so, please state your wife's full name, and her maiden name.
Answer: Yes Mary Jane Elizabeth Howel

No. 2. When, where, and by whom were you married? Answer: December 30– 1885 Rev Henry Williams Pleasent Ridge A.M.E. Church, Ballard Co Ky

No. 3. What record of marriage exists? Answer: I cannot say as I am not familar with the law Touching such

No. 4. Were you previously married? If so, please state the name of your former wife and the date and place of her death or divorce. Answer: I was to Rebecca Neal died died Nov 24– 1885 in Ballard Co Ky 4 miles N.W. of Lovelaceville Ky who

No. 5. Have you any children living? If so, please state their names and the dates of their birth. Answer: William Pleasant was borned Jany 12 1867
Salvany was borned Jany 22 1869
Mary Jane was borned Aug 2 1871
Horrance Lee was borned Feby 17 1873
Isom McDaniel May 2 1875

Date of reply, October 18, 1897.

Isam Washington
(Signature)

[Stamp: PENSION OFFICE U.S. OCT 21 1897]

Figure 17. Isam Washington's pension application.

Elizabeth (Howell) Washington

Searching the Massac Co., IL 1910 Census for Washingtons, we found Elizabeth Washington living in Brookport, listed as Widow, age 70. Since her age was listed as 50 in the 1900 Census in Ballard Co., KY, her age is off by 10 years, because there was no other Elizabeth Washington found in the county. Discrepancies in ages from one census year to another are common for all persons, but especially with the ages of Blacks.

1910 CENSUS: Brookport, Massac, IL ED 70 Sheet 7B:
146-153 WASHINGTON, Elizabeth Head 70 Wd Mother of 7 children 2 living
KY KY KY

Her birthplace was listed KY. Living nearby was her stepson Horace Washington. This information and the Civil War pension files document that Elizabeth was the widow of Isham/Isam Washington, who died in Massac Co., IL in 1903. Remember, a census does not absolutely, positively document a birth or marriage or the number of children born to a woman. For example, on the 1900 census Mary Jane Elizabeth (Howell) Frasier Washington gave her age as 50 and said she was the mother of three children, all three of whom were then living. Ten years later, on the 1910 census she gave her age as 70 and reported that she had had seven children, two of whom were then living. One must ask the question, if it is possible or even probable that she had four children born to her during her 50s. More than likely, she did have seven children in all but only three of them were living in 1900. The records show she had two living (surviving) children during her marriage with Woodson Frasier (tax records state two children were living in his home). A third child we know of was Schooler G. Washington, her son with Isam/Isham Washington; Schooler G. was found on the 1900 census in their household. Obviously, additional research is necessary to find out how many children she did have and when and where they died.

Isam's Children:

Sallie Washington. Beginning the search with the known, Marriage Book B, pages 112-113, of Ballard Co., Ky. list a marriage record for Sallie Washington and John Stahl in 1886. Sallie was listed as a surviving sister in Isam Mack D. Washington's obituary. Isham also named Sallie in his pension file as one of his living children. With these clues a census search was made for John and Sallie (Washington) Stahl in Ballard Co., finding them in both the 1900 and 1910 U.S. Census.

1900 CENSUS: BALLARD COUNTY, KY, PAGE 48:
Stahl, John   Head Black Male   1860 age 40 Married 15 years Born Ky
  "   Sallie   Wife   "   Female Jan 1870 age 30 Married 15 yrs Born Ky
  "   Martha S Dau   "   Female Jul 1883 age 16 Single   Born Ky
  "   Florence Dau   "   Female Aug 1887 age 12 Single   Born Ky

1910 CENSUS: BALLARD COUNTY, KY, ED. No. 1, page 5A, 87-88:
Stahl, John   Black, Male, age 48, farmer, 1st Marriage,   Born KY
Stahl, Sallie   " , Female, " 38,   1st Marriage,   Born KY
                           Sallie's father Born: Unknown
                                   mother Born: Unknown

William P. Washington. Also, records show that William P. Washington was in Ballard Co., in 1887, evidence, he was found in Mortgage Book F (see Table 4). William P. was not found in Ballard Co., in the 1900 Census — only Isham and Mack D. were found there. It is suspected that William P. left Ballard Co. before 1900 and migrated to Massac Co., Illinois, where Isam and Mack D. migrated too after 1900. Searching the 1900 Census in Massac Co., Illinois, finding William and his wife Georgia living in Brooklyn Precinct. Searching all the county, finding only a Nettie Washington, stepdaughter of a ___ Matthew. No other Washington was found living there. Examining the Census closely revealed that William was born in Kentucky, January 1867 (exact date found in earlier records — his father born in NC, his mother in KY).

1900 CENSUS: Brooklyn Precinct, Village of Brooklyn, Massac, IL ED 48
    Sheet 14B:
Washington, William, head, Jan 1867 33 M 13yrs KY NC KY minister
    Georgia, wife, --- 1865 35 M 13yrs KY KY KY cannot read/write
                    mother of 7 children — 5 living
    Howard,   Armade, step dau, Jan 1883 17 S   KY KY KY
              Ardie, dau, May 1887 13 S   KY KY KY
              Eva, dau, Jan 1889 11 S   KY KY KY
              Exey, dau, Mar 1896 4 S   KY KY KY
              William, son, Mar 1894 6 S   IL KY KY

He was 33 years old and had been married 13 years. His occupation was listed minister. His wife Georgia, age 35, married 13 years, mother of seven children, five living. All were born in Kentucky except William Jr., the youngest, the only child born in Illinois, March 1894. The birth of his youngest child is evidence that William left Kentucky sometime before 1894.

Also found in the 1910 Census was Georgia Washington, listed as Widow, but there is evidence that William Washington was not dead. A search of Massac Co. vital records for William's death record was unsuccessful. Second, family information tells that Isom M.D. Washington was in Decatur, IL in 1922. A search of the 1921-22 Decatur directories disclosed Rev. William P. Washington, pastor, Antioch Baptist Church, living at 600 Greenwood Ave. The following year (1922) Booker T., Elizabeth, Isom M.D., and William P. Washington were living on Greenwood Ave. in Decatur, Ill. Three years later 1925 (see Figure 18) the Washingtons were still residents of Decatur.

Documents found indicate that William P. and Isom M.D. Washington were brothers and ministers; there is evidence that William P. Washington was not deceased (in 1910) but living in Decatur, Ill. as late as 1925. Other Washington family records found in Massac County, Ill.: Isom M.D. and Arbella Washington's marriage record; Isam Washington's death record; and Booker T. Washington's birth record.

Learning more about Isam Washington in the 1870s and 1880s

A careful perusal of the local newspapers available in Ballard County should give information about the goings-on in the area where he lived and raised his children. We can learn from the published Ballard County, Kentucky history books about the concerns of the residents and those issues which they thought were significant enough to include in their county's history.

When the family history researcher reads a nineteenth century county history book for the county where his forebears lived, a bridge begins to take form to unite the twentieth century descendant with the lives and times of his ancestors and their friends and neighbors. Most likely, not every ancestor will be mentioned in the county history, but we can still learn about the usual and unusual happenings in the area where our forebears lived.

The Origin of Isam Washington's Surname

One question which many descendants of former slaves wonder is, how did Great-Grandfather choose the family surname? It appears highly unlikely Isam chose Washington from one of his owners. Why? Well, for one thing, it is interesting to note that there were no other Washington families living in Ballard County, either Black or White, in the early 1860s. Two well-known authors in the field of genealogy have made statements on how ex-slaves chose their surnames after the Civil War. In *Black Genealogy*, by Black historian and genealogist Charles Blackson, with journalist Ron Fry: "freed blacks . . . frequently threw off their slave names and adopted whatever 'free' names they fancied, producing a flood of George Washingtons and Thomas Jeffersons.[91]" The most popular surnames adopted by ex-slaves after emancipation were Lincoln and Washington, says John Cerny, author of "Black Ancestral Research" in *Source*.[92] We can speculate that Isam probably chose the name Washington because that was

---

[91] Charles Blockson and Ron Fry, *Black Genealogy* (Englewood Cliffs, NJ: Prentice-Hall, Inc., 1977), p. 4.

[92] John Cerny, "Black ancestral research," in *Source* (Salt Lake City, UT: Ancestry Publication, 1985), p. 579.

NORMAN LAUNDRY & DRY CLEANING CO.
Quality Laundering and Expert Cleaning
PHONE M. 3800
PLANT 115 PROSPECT AVE.
OFFICE 230 N. MAIN

MAYTAG WASHING MACHINES AND MANGLES

CARL H. NYE
FORMERLY HARRIS MODERN HEATING CO.
216 E. NORTH STREET
OIL BURNERS — WATER SOFTENERS — ELECTRIC REFRIGERATORS

DECATUR CITY DIRECTORY   463

arren Cleta M, opr Ill Bell Tel, r 522 E Johnson av.
rren Donald E (Jean), baggageman Wabash, r 1242½ E Eldorado.
rren D Elmer (Lillian), (Warren The Tailor), r 1062 W Prairie av.
rren Edwin, r 1287 E Vanderhoof.
rren Elizabeth, r 1111 N Warren.
rren George H (Sylvia), grocer 1240 N Broadway, r 522 E Johnson av.
rren Green B, wks Mueller, rms 500 E Central av.
rren Harvey D (Anna M), r 518½ N Water.
rren Irene, tchr, r 31 W Fairview pl.
rren James, meat ctr W H F Vahrenholdt, r 558 N East av.
rren James P, carp, r 558 N East av.
rren John E (Grace), hoseman Fire Station No 1, r 218 W Cerro Gordo.
rren John H (Mildred), office mgr sales dept Staley, r 1061 W Prairie.
rren Lee E (Jennie), ship clk Home Mfg, r 520 E Olive.
rren Leota E, opr Ill Bell Tel, r 522 E Johnson av.
rren Lewis H (Bertha C), real est, 31 W Fairview pl.
rren Mattie (col), r 640 W Marietta.
rren Milton G (Bernice), clk Wilder & Wilder, r Montgomery pl 1st w of Dennis av.
rren Naomi, r 1111 N Warren.
rren Paul L (Bertha), clk Saltz Bros, 1065 E Moore.
rren Street School, Nelle N Clark prin, 1419 N Water.
rren Tedwell T (Mary), pipe ftr Wabash, r 1635 N Walnut Grove av.
rren The Tailor (D E Warren, Alex Kazmark), 163 E Prairie av.
rren Wm L, metal wkr Walrus Mfg, 548 N East av.
rren Willis D P (Anna E), (Holbrook, Warren & Van Praag), r 145 N Haworth av.
scher Harry F, wks C B Q Co, r 1239 E Marietta.
sen Armand (Augusta), wks Ill Traction, r 728 W Cushing.
shburn Aden R (Florence), lab, r 131 S Broadway.
shburn Anna J, r 823 S Webster.
shburn Arthur (Mae), tmstr, r 2821 E Main.
shburn Clara M (wid J P), r 2023 N Woodford.
shburn David H (Celia), grinder Mueller, r 816 N Pine.
shburn Elizabeth (wid Nathan), nurse, r 1027 W Green.
shburn Fritz L (Marian C), civil eng, 401 E 5th.
shburn Isabell E (wid J W), r 823 S Webster.
shburn James R (Helen), com trav, 816 E Johns av.
shburn Noah D, r 823 S Webster.
shburn Ralph, r 2023 N Woodford.
shek Albert H, r 340 E Wabash av.

Washek Amos A, driver Danzeisen Pkg, r 862 S 6th.
Washek Marie, r 340 E Wabash av.
Washington Booker T (col), janitor Frede & Son, r 540 S Greenwood av.
Washington Guy (col), wks Cadillac Co, r 503 Greenwood av.
Washington Isom M D Rev (col) (Arbelle), pastor St Peter's A M E Church, r 540 S Greenwood av.
Washington Lucine (col), elevator opr Linn & Scruggs, r 1005 W St Louis av.
Washington Plumer (col) (Lulu), lab, r 580 S Franklin.
Washington Wm P Rev (col) (Eliza), r 1005 W St Louis av.
Washington Wm P jr (Lucine), porter Gushard, r 1005 W St Louis av.
WASH-RITE LAUNDRY CORP, L H Smith pres; C W Nunn sec; rear 535 N Water phone M-1229.
Wassen Louis, lineman Ill Power, r 2040 W William.
Wasson Charles L (Lulu M), photog 5th fl D Drug Bldg, r 855 W Eldorado.
Wasson Joseph L, car repr Wabash, r 516 E Orchard.
Wasson Mollie, wks Williams Scaling, r 426 E Main.
Wasson Oddy C (Ella), eng Wabash, r 1344 E William.
Wasson Van R jr (Cora), mach Cash Co, r 1432 W Forest av.
Wastel Carlos, clk Wabash, r 1129 N Clinton.
Wastel Joseph A (Thelma), wks D Mal Iron, r 1129 N Clinton.
Waterland Eliza (wid Henry), r 1537 N Water.
Waters Daniel W (Doris M), tmstr, r 2676 E Cerro Gordo.
Waters Ferne D, thr Roach Sch, r 1505 N Monroe.
Watford John (ol) (Sarah), wks Wagner Iron, r 1440 E Sangamon.
Watkins Alice E, stenog Ill Standard Trust, r 1089 S Broadway.
Watkins Arthur W (Lucille), elect Staley, r 405 E Waggoner.
Watkins Charles M, wks Staley, r 1089 S Broadway.
Watkins Eber T (Eliza), wks Ill Power, r 1256 E Dickinson av.
Watkins Edna Mrs, opr Ill Bell Tel, r 174 N 6th.
Watkins Edward (Emma), cook Wm Watkins, r 561 N College.
Watkins Erastus M (col), fireman Simon Bernstein, r 635 S Greenwood av.
Watkins Ernest S (Lela), molder Mueller, r 2446 E Main.
Watkins Forrest, ook Knowles & Guynn, r 240 N Park av.
Watkins Frank (Edna), wks Staley, r 174 N 6th.
Watkins Henry W (Jessie), molder Mueller, r 2419 E William.
Watkins Iulous G (col) (Bessie), fireman Water Wks, r 520 S Greenwood av.

arehouse and Yards 541 Wabash Avenue   Tracks, Wabash and C. I. & W. Railways
SIMON BURSTEIN
WHOLESALE AND RETAIL
IDES, PELTS, WOOL, FURS, TALLOW, RAGS, RUBBER, PAPER, METALS, OLD IRON, TAILOR CLIPS, GINSENG
hone Main 1364   Paper Stock a Specialty

Figure 18. Decatur, Illinois city directory.

the name of the first president of the United States. We learned from the land and census records that Isam could write and read, which leads to the conclusion that he may have read about George Washington in addition to hearing about him. Obviously, more research into the early life of Isam Washington is needed to learn about his life and possibly his parents' lives as slaves. Also, a search into his later life is needed. It is as yet unknown how the several Washingtons in Ballard County fitted into the Isam family. Of the Washington marriages in Ballard County, Kentucky about the time Isam/Isham's children would have been of marrying age, it is not now known whether or not these other Washingtons were his children. It does not appear that there was another Washington family in the area, but there are no clues as to who were the other Washingtons mentioned in the marriage registers.

But for now this researcher feels a sense of accomplishment in tracing Harold Washington's pedigree back to his great-grandfather, Isam Washington, who was born in North Carolina in 1832.

Massac County Vital Records: Arbella (Hamilton) Weeks's Genealogy

At this point in the Washington ancestor research, no marriage record for Mack and Arbella had been found. A search of Massac Co. vital records provided the researcher with a Register of Marriage entry for Mack and Arbella. This register revealed genealogical information of importance. Most of the information in the record matches previously known facts about Mack's parents and birthplaces. Arbella's parents were named for the first time in this record. (See Figure 19.) However, the maiden name of Arbella Hamilton and Smith Weeks, the name of her alleged father, didn't agree; therefore more evidence was needed to substantiate a father-and-daughter relationship. The most important discrepancy to be noted is Arbella's birthplace: her Missouri death record provides her birthplace as Mexico, Mo.; the 1910 Census lists it as Illinois, and the 1900 Census lists it as Kentucky; on her marriage register her birthplace is given as Mississippi County.

To establish Arbella Hamilton's birthplace and her parents name, a census search was conducted. In a search of the 1880 Illinois Soundex for Smith Weeks, the name was not found. Next, the 1900 Census of Massac Co. Illinois and of Brooklyn was searched for any Hamilton family, or any names appearing on marriage licenses. We found the family of Sep Hamilton with wife Lizzie and daughter Lida.

Register Of Marriages, Massac County, Illinois

1. NO. OF LICENSE 2. DATE OF LICENSE	1. 3822 2. 8/8/96			
1. BY WHOM AFFIDAVIT, IF ANY IS MADE 2. By Whom Consent to Marriage Given	1. 2.			
1. FULL NAME OF GROOM 2. PLACE OF RESIDENCE 3. OCCUPATION	1. Mack Washington 2. Ballard Co., KY 3. Farming	1. AGE NEXT BIRTHDAY 2. RACE OR COLOR 3. PLACE OF BIRTH	1. 22 YEARS 2. B. African 3. Ballard Co., Kentucky	1. FATHER'S NAME 2. MOTHER'S MAIDEN NAME 3. NO. OF GROOM'S MARRIAGE	1. Isom Washington 2. Rebecca Washington 3. 1
1. FULL NAME OF BRIDE 2. MAIDEN NAME, IF A WIDOW 3. PLACE OF RESIDENCE	1. Arbella Hamilton 2. B. 3. Miss. Co. Brooklyn, Massac Co.	1. AGE NEXT BIRTHDAY 2. RACE OR COLOR 3. PLACE OF BIRTH	1. 19 YEARS 2. African 3.	1. FATHER'S NAME 2. MOTHER'S MAIDEN NAME 3. NO. OF BRIDE'S MARRIAGE	1. Smith Weeks 2. Elizabeth Robinson 3. 1
1. WHERE AND WHEN MARRIED 2. WITNESSES 3. BY WHOM CERTIFIED, NAME AND OFFICE	1. AT Metropolis Aug. 8 1896 2. Lide Hamilton, Billy Green 3. H. Vaudenburg	1. DATE OF RETURN 2. WHEN REGISTERED	1. 08-10-1896 2. 01/1897		

STATE OF ILLINOIS
Massac County } ss.   Illinois

I, ... John Oldham ...., County Clerk of said County and State aforesaid, do hereby certify that the record herewith certified is a true and complete copy of the certificate of the marriage of .... Mack Washington ....
and .... Arbella Hamilton .... as the same appears of record in my office.

WITNESS my hand and the seal of County Court of said County at .... Massac ....
this .... 5th .... day of .... September .... A.D. 19.. 91 ....

By ....*John Oldham*.......... County Clerk,
.... *Irene Williams* .... Deputy

Figure 19. Marriage register of Mack Washington and Arbella Weeks.

77

```
1900 CENSUS: Brooklyn, Massac, IL, ED 48 Sheet 16, 25 June
Hamilton, Sep  head b a Mar 1848 52 married 23yrs           KY KY KY
          Lizzie wife b f     1847 53 married 23yrs 7-6 kids TN TN TN
          Lula  dau  b f Apr 1877 23 single                 AR KY TN
          Lida  dau  b f Feb 1879 21 single                 IL KY TN
          Boid  son  b m Apr 1881 19 single                 IL KY TN
          Wade  son  b m Jan 1883 17 single                 IL KY TN
          Uren  son  b m Apr 1887 13 single                 IL KY TN
          Bryant son b m Apr 1891 11 single                 IL KY TN
```

In 1896, Lida Hamilton was one of the witnesses to the marriage of Arbella Hamilton and Mack Washington. The 1900 Census identifies Lida's parents as Sep and Lizzie Hamilton. Calculating Arbella's age from her marriage record, she should have been approximately 2 years old and living with her parents in 1880. These clues led to a 1880 Census search of Massac Co., Illinois for Sep and Lizzie Hamilton, finding them in Brooklyn, with daughters Lidey and "Ibeller" both born in Arkansas.

```
1880 Census: Brooklyn, Massac, IL, ED 62, Sheet 55 8 June
Hamilton, Sip    b m 28      married Laborer                KY KY KY
   Elizzie  b f 29 wife married Keeps house can't read/write KY -- -
   Joseph   b m 12 son  single              "    "    "     KY KY KY
   Louley   b f  4 dau  single                              KY KY KY
   Ibeller  b f  2 dau  single                              ARK KY KY
   Lidey E  b f 5/12 dau single                             ARK KY KY
```

Arbella's name is spelled "Ibeller" which is a common phonic variation found in census records. Searching the entire county in Jackson Township, the family of Samuel and Carolin Hamilton with Mary R. listed as mother was found.

```
1880 CENSUS: Jackson, Massac, IL, ED 62 Sheet 7, 16 June 1880
Hamilton, Samuel  b m 56, farmer, married  can't read/write KY KY KY
        Carolin   b f 52, wife, married    can't read/write NC NC NC
        Marry Ros b f 80, mother, widowed  can't read       NC NC NC
        Nelley J  b f 13, daugh, single,   can't read/write IL NC NC
        Albert    b m 12, son, single      can't read/write KY NC NC
        Jesse     b m 12, step, single     can't      write IL NC NC
        Warren H  b m  9, son, single                       IL NC NC
```

To return to Arbella Hamilton's marriage record, she said her birthplace was Mississippi County, no state listed. The Webster's Geographical Dictionary shows Mississippi counties in both Arkansas and Missouri. The Kentucky map shows Mississippi Co., Missouri right across the river from Ballard Co., Ky. The logical place to search next was the Missouri Soundex for Smith Weeks in Mississippi Co., Mo. A search of the 1880 Census was conducted, with negative result.

A birth record for Arbella could have provided direct evidence of who her parents were. Unfortunately the Mississippi Co. Courthouse, Blytheville, Ark., had no such record. However there is strong evidence that Smith Weeks and Elizabeth Robinson were the parents of Arbella, and her birthplace was Mississippi Co., Arkansas. Based on clues and evidence, it appears that Smith Weeks and Elizabeth Robinson were married for a short time and Arbella and her older sister were children born to this marriage. When Smith Weeks died, it appears that Sep Hamilton married the widow Elizabeth (Robinson) Weeks and raised her two daughters as his own.

Presently no certificate or other documentation of Elizabeth's first marriage to Smith Weeks has been found: therefore the conclusion is based on three supporting pieces of evidence: (1) the statement given in the census that Sep's marriage to Elizzie was his second, and that Elizzie's marriage to Sep was her second; (2) the statement given by Arbella on her marriage license application that her father was Smith Weeks and her mother was Elizabeth Robinson; (3) Arbella said her birthplace was Arkansas and her maiden name was Weeks in her third child Booker T.'s birth record, found in Massac Co., IL courthouse. Other clues suggest they were both previously married to others. First, the 1880 census enumeration lists Sep's son Joseph as being 12 years old or born in about 1868 and the 1900 census reports Sep had been married for 23 years to Elizzie or since about 1877. Therefore, with preponderant evidence it is concluded that Arbella D. Weeks's parents were Smith Weeks and Elizabeth Robinson, Sep Hamilton was her adopted or stepfather, and her birthplace was Mississippi Co., Ark.

Extending the research of the Hamilton family, the 1910 Census of Massac Co., Illinois was also searched finding Sep and Lizzie Hamilton in Brooklyn Precinct. Living next door were Samuel and Carolin Hamilton (probably the parents). In the same dwelling as Sip and Lizzie is the family of Lydia Wheeler (probably Lida Hamilton) with Horace Washington as boarder.

1910 CENSUS: Brooklyn Precinct, Brookport City, Massac, IL ED 70 Sheet 8A:
```
Hamilton, Samuel head 84 M1 45yrs KY KY KY
          Carolin wife  82 M2 45yrs NC NC NC (10-5 kids)
     Warren   son   35 Wd       IL KY NC
     Jesse    son   42 Wd       IL KY NC
     Daniel   son   11 S        IL IL IL possibly the son of Jesse
     McGowan  son   10 S        IL IL IL     "   "   "   "   "
Taylor, Maud boarder 17 S       TN TN TN
Next household:
    Hamilton, Sip head  60 M  31yrs IL KY NC
              Lizzie wife 56 M 31yrs IL IL IL (10-6 kids)
         Boyd son   28 S       IL IL IL
    Wheeler, Lydia head 30 Wd       IL IL IL (2-2 kids)
```

```
            Ethel     dau      6 S        IL IL IL
            Prentess  son      4 S        IL IL IL
   Washington, Horace boarder 35 S        KY KY KY
```

Based on the 1910 Census entries, Samuel and Carolin Hamilton are primary candidates for Sep's parents, but in genealogy one cannot assume a parent-and-child relationship — it must be established by clues and evidence. A careful study of Massac County 1910 and 1880 censuses provides circumstantial evidence and clues to identify Samuel and Carolin as parents of Sep Hamilton. First Samuel and Sep were the only Black families found living in the County in 1910. Second, they were living next door to each other. Third, Samuel and Carolin's birthplaces match with the said birthplaces of Sep's father and mother. On the 1910 Census, Sep's birthplace and his parents' birthplaces are listed as Kentucky. This discrepancy in the Census will need further research to identify Sep's birthplace. Moving back 30 years (1880) Samuel and Sep are the only Black families found in Massac Co. Samuel and Carolin's birthplaces match. Their ages are slightly off, but not significantly. Living in the same household is Mary Rose, age 80, listed as mother. Based on the census information, it is believed that Mary Rose was the mother of Carolin, not Samuel. Samuel said on the 1880 census that his mother was born in KY, and although he gave the relationship of "mother" to her, Mary Rose gave her birthplace as NC. Furthermore, Samuel's second wife, Carolin, said *her* mother was born in NC. Obviously, additional research is necessary to find out whose mother was Mary R.

Reviewing the evidence and clues to who-was-who in the Sep Hamilton family given in the 1880, 1900 and 1910 censuses, the following comes to light:

(1) Sep was married first to Miss _____ (name presently unknown) probably around 1865-68. They had at least one child, a son they named Joseph. Sep's first wife died, or they were divorced, prior to 1878.

(2) Elizabeth Robinson was first married to Smith Weeks who records indicate was the father of Arbella. He was probably also the father of Elizabeth's daughter Louley, b. about 1875-76, who was older than Arbella (see the 1880 census). Smith Weeks probably died about 1878.

(3) Sep Hamilton married Elizabeth (Robinson) Weeks early in 1879. Their marriage probably took place sometime between January and April, evidence that Lidey was born January 1880.

On the 1900 census enumeration for Sep and Lizzie we see that Lizzie reported she was the mother of seven children, six of whom were then living. Counting the children living with them at that time, the total is six: Lula, Lida, Boid [sic], Wade, Uren and Bryant. Arbella was married by then, so the total known number of children born to Lizzie was seven. Why then did she say she had had seven children but only six were then living? Perhaps she misinterpreted the question to mean, how many of your children are living *with you*.

By the 1910 census, Sep and Lizzie had only one child living with them, their son Boyd. At that time Lizzie reported she had ten children, but only 6 were then living. We assume that she had had three more children born to her and Sep between 1900 and 1910 and that they had probably buried four of their children. A search of the death and cemetery records for Massac County should provide the researcher with the information about these additional children.

Also on the 1910 census, notice that Sep lived next door to his parents and that he had living in his household his widowed daughter, Lydia, and her two children, Ethel and Prentice, plus Horace Washington, the brother-in-law of his daughter, Arbella [i.e. his son-in-law Isom McDaniel Washington's brother]. This suggests that the Hamiltons and Washingtons were a close family who could rely upon one another.

This concludes the census study of Arbella D. (Weeks) Hamilton Washington's family. This Census provided the researcher with supporting evidence that Arbella's parents were Smith Weeks and Elizabeth Robinson, and Sep Hamilton was most likely her adopted or stepfather. Isham Washington's death record was also found in Massac Co. vital records, providing the researcher with new genealogical information. It was learned from this record that he was a minister and died of heart failure at the age of 73, 27 June 1903 in Brookport, Illinois. It was learned from Booker Washington's birth record, found in Massac Co., that he was the third child, born 22 Sept. 1904 to Mack and Arbella Washington, and that Arbella listed her maiden name as Weeks, not Hamilton, in the record. She also gave her birthplace as Arkansas, which matches the information in her marriage record.

This concludes the study of Isham/Isam Washington Civil War pension records which have revealed genealogical and historical information in Ballard Co., Ky. and extended this search to Massac Co., Ill. This data has documented his life from 1864-1903.

Conclusion

We must keep in mind as we research our ancestors' lives that they were human, just as we are. They had trials and experiences which brought about the same emotions which we have felt or would feel were we in much the same situations. They lived and loved. They married, they buried their loved ones. They went off to war, they stayed home and worried and prayed for their husbands, sons and brothers. They planted and harvested and then preserved their foods. They nursed their sick and cried over their losses through death, disease or distance of family members, neighbors, animals or crops. They rejoiced when a pregnancy did not cost the life of the mother or her babe. And when it did, they comforted those who had to carry on with broken hearts. They may not have had the same creature comforts we enjoy today, but their lives were rich in experiences that molded their characters and values and which have been passed on down from generation to generation and which we have inherited. When we look closely at our own pedigree, what do we see? We see ourselves.

APPENDIX A

A BRIEF HISTORY OF BALLARD COUNTY

A Brief History of Ballard County

Ballard County, where the earliest known ancestor of Harold Washington was found, is one of eight western Kentucky counties which form that part of the state known as the Jackson Purchase. Bound by the Mississippi and Tennessee river, the region originally belonged to the Chickasaw Indian Nation, but the United States government purchased it in 1818.[93] The county is bounded on the north by the Ohio River, on the west by the Mississippi River, on the east by McCracken County, and on the south by Hickman County.

Ballard County was formed as a county in 1842. It was once a part of Hickman and McCracken counties. The original county seat was in Blandville until Feb. 1880 when the courthouse burned with many records lost. The present county seat is in Wickliff, Kentucky. Ballard County citizens' primary source of income was farming. In 1870, according to the "Ballard County, Ky. Historical Overview," over two million pounds of tobacco were produced in the county and nearly five hundred bushels of wheat. Also, livestock such as hogs, cattle, horses, and mules were very important to Ballard Co. citizens.

The county population statistics for Whites, free colored, and slaves for 1850, -60, and -70 were:

	White	Free Colored	Slave
1850	4,628	0	842
1860	6,943	31	1718
1870	11,099	1,477	0[94]

The records show that three generations of Harold Washington's ancestors were residents of Ballard County in 1900.

---

[93] Philip M. Cochran, "A historical overview of Ballard County" (Frankfort, KY, Kentucky Historical Society, 1978), p. 2.

[94] Ibid., Population, from 1850-1870 (1873 ed.), p. 258.

APPENDIX B

CIVILIAN CONSERVATION CORPS RECORDS OF HAROLD LEE WASHINGTON

1. Certificate of Selection

2. Designation of Allottee

3. Individual Record

4. Record of Service

5. Discharge Records

negro

CERTIFICATE OF SELECTION
for the
CIVILIAN CONSERVATION CORPS

006-269313

Date: JUL 7 1939

APPLICANT'S NAME: WASHINGTON, Harold Lee
(Last Name) (First Name) (Middle)
ADDRESS: 111 E. 64th St.
POST OFFICE: Chicago
STATE OF ILLINOIS COUNTY: Cook

Application Received By
LOCAL AGENCY: Illinois Emergency Relief Commission
ADDRESS: Civilian Conservation Corps, Cook County Selecting Office, 1257 No. Paulina Street
CITY or TOWN: Chicago, Illinois

SECTION 1.

Age: 17 Place and date of birth: Chicago, Ill. April 15 1922
(City and State) (Month) (Day) (Year)

If not born in the United States, have you been naturalized? ___ First papers ___ (Date) ___ Final papers ___ (Place) ___ (Date)

Height: 68¼ Weight: 158 Color of eyes: brown Color of hair: brown
(Minimum: 60 in.) (Minimum: 107 lb.)

Applicant's Marital Status: single Is your father living? yes Mother living? yes
(Yes or No) (Yes or No)

How many brothers? 2 Sisters 1 Occupation of principal wage earner of family: lawyer

How many members of your family reside in the same household with you? (Excluding applicant) 5
(Number)

Do you live on a farm? no If so, is the farm owned by your family? ___
(Yes or No) (Yes or No)

Do you live in a town or village of less than 2500 persons, or in a rural area, and not on a farm? no
(Yes or No)

School last attended: Du Sable High Sch. Located at: Chicago, Ill. Date of leaving: 3/1/39
(Name of School) (City and State)

EDUCATION: (Circle highest grade completed)
GRAMMAR OR GRADE SCHOOL 1 2 3 4 5 6 7 8
HIGH SCHOOL 1 2 3 4 COLLEGE 1 2 3 4

Special educational or vocational interests: auto mechanics

Applicant's reason(s) for desiring C.C.C. enrollment: need employment

SECTION 2.

Are you now unemployed? yes How long unemployed? 10 Do you need employment? yes
(Yes or No) (Months) (Yes or No)

Have you ever had a paid regular job? yes If so, give date last job ended: 2/6/39
(Yes or No)

Eligible for unemployment compensation? no Receiving such compensation? ___ If not, is claim pending? ___
(Yes or No) (Yes or No) (Yes or No)

Registered with State Employment Service? yes Work best qualified for: common labor
(Yes or No)

If previously employed, give chronological statement of your work history in space below:

Name and address of Employer	Name of work performed	Inclusive Dates of Employment From	To
1. Chelsea pharmacy	porter	July	Sept.
2. Laplette Food Mart	clerk	Dec. '1937	June '38

1. Certificate of Selection

89

Previously enrolled in the Civilian Conservation Corps? No   Former individual serial number _____
(Yes or No)

List all previous service below:

Company Number	Length of Service (Months) (Days)	Date Enrolled	Date Discharged	Type of Discharge (Hon. Adm. or Dishon.)

Total length of all previous service in Civilian Conservation Corps: Months _____ Days _____

SECTION 4.   DESIGNATION OF ALLOTTEE

(Required for all juniors having dependents. Juniors without dependents will use Section 5.)

Allotment from Monthly Cash Allowance desired by applicant to be made to dependent(s) as follows:

Name: WASHINGTON, Roy   Relationship: Father
(Last Name) (First) (Middle)

Address: 111 E. 44th Street, Chicago, Ill.   Amount: $22.00

Name: _____
(Last Name) (First) (Middle)   Relationship: _____

Address: _____   Amount: _____

In addition to allotment, applicant desires deposit in the sum of $ _____ per month.

SECTION 5.   AUTHORIZATION ... IT IN LIEU OF ALLOTMENT

Completion of _____ (All cases in which Section 4 is not used.)

I. FROM THE SELECTING AGENCY: It is hereby ... Civilian Conservation Corps effective July 1, 1937, that the ... been obtained that he does not have any dependent member or ... to be selected and enrolled in the Corps he is therefore required to agree to make a monthly deposit of pay in the amount of $ _____ with the Chief of Finance, War Department, to be repaid normally upon completion of or release from enrollment.

... suant to regulations issued under Section 9 of the Act to establish ... verification of the status of the applicant named herein, proper assurance ... members of his family to whom an allotment of pay can be made. ...

Selecting Agent's Signature _____

II. FROM THE APPLICANT: In accordance with the aforementioned Act and regulations prescribed thereunder by the Director of the Corps, I hereby certify that I do not have any dependent member or members of my family to whom an allotment of pay can be made, and I agree to make a monthly deposit of pay with the Chief of Finance, War Department, in the amount specified above, to be repaid normally upon completion of or release from enrollment.

Applicant's signature _____

SECTION 6.

The statements contained in the foregoing Sections are true, to the best of my knowledge. I desire to be enrolled in the Civilian Conservation Corps for a period of six months unless earlier released in accord with law and established regulations. If I am accepted and enrolled, I agree to abide faithfully by the rules and regulations of the Corps and am willing to be assigned to any C.C.C. camp within the continental United States.

Applicant's Signature (ink): Harold Lee Washington

SECTION 7.   CIVILIAN CONSERVATION CORPS

_____ CERTIFIES that the above named applicant has been properly selected for enrollment as a Junior in the Civilian Conservation Corps. On completion of his enrollment, including physical examination, he has been directed to report to U.S. Army authorities at _____ NEW POSTOFFICE BLDG.

on JUL 7 1939, 1939, at _____ A.M. / P.M.

ILLINOIS EMERGENCY RELIEF COMMISSION
222 W. North Bank Drive,
Chicago, Illinois.
LEO. M. LYONS Executive Secretary

By _____ Otto Kreuzer

JUL 7 1939

To Army

2. Designation of Allottee

INDIVIDUAL RECORD
CIVILIAN CONSERVATION CORPS

I. GENERAL INFORMATION

ILLINOIS

Serial No. CC-6-269313

1. Name: WASHINGTON HAROLD LEE
2. Address: 111 E. 44th St. Chicago, Ill
3. Date of birth: April 15, 1922
4. Birthplace: Chicago, Illinois
5. Nearest relative: Roy Washington 111 E. 44th St Chicago, Illinois Father
6. Citizenship: Native born
7. Color: Coloured
8. Military or naval service: None
9. Height: 63½" Weight: 168 Complexion: dark Color of hair: black
   Color of eyes: brown Scars or identifying marks: none
10. Education (circle highest grade completed): Grammar school, 1 2 3 4 5 6 7 8; high school, 1 (2) 3 4; college, 1 2 3 4;
    other education: None
11. Occupational qualifications: Laborer

Occupation		Length of experience
Obriens Pharmacy	Porter	July to September
Duplatta Food Mart	Clerk	Dec.'37 to June '38

12. Were you previously a member of the Civilian Conservation Corps? No

Company	Location	Enrolled	Discharged	Character of discharge

II. OATH OF ENROLLMENT

I, Harold Lee Washington, do solemnly swear (or affirm) that the information given above as to my status is correct. I agree to remain in the Civilian Conservation Corps for the period terminating at the discretion of the United States between July 8, 1939 to December 31, 1939 unless sooner released by proper authority, and that I will obey those in authority and observe all the rules and regulations thereof to the best of my ability and will accept such allowances as may be provided pursuant to law and regulations promulgated pursuant thereto. I understand and agree that any injury received or disease contracted by me while a member of the Civilian Conservation Corps cannot be made the basis of any claim against the Government, except such as I may be entitled to under the act of February 15, 1934 (48 Stat. 351; U. S. C. 5: 796), and that I shall not be entitled to any allowances upon release from camp, except transportation in kind to the place at which I was accepted for enrollment. I understand further that any articles issued to me by the United States Government for use while a member of the Civilian Conservation Corps are, and remain, property of the United States Government and that willful destruction, loss, sale, or disposal of such property renders me financially responsible for the cost thereof and liable to trial in the civil courts. I understand further that any infraction of the rules or regulations of the Civilian Conservation Corps renders me liable to expulsion therefrom. So help me God.

CCC Company 660
Camp Bitely F-22 (Mich)
Bitely, Michigan

Signature: Harold Lee Washington

Sworn to and subscribed before me this 8th day of July, nineteen hundred and thirty 9

F. L. Samson, 1st Lt. Inf-Res. Enrolling Officer

3. Individual Record

III. REENROLLMENTS

Company _____ Camp _____ Date _____

I accept reenrollment in the Civilian Conservation Corps for the period ending at the discretion of the United States between _____ under the same conditions as my previous enrollment.

_____
(Enrollee's signature)

Reenrolled this _____ day of _____, 193___

Signature _____

_____
(Name, grade, and organization, typed or stamped) Company Commander.

Company _____ Camp _____ Date _____

I accept reenrollment in the Civilian Conservation Corps for the period ending at the discretion of the United States between _____ under the same conditions as my previous enrollment.

_____
(Enrollee's signature)

Reenrolled this _____ day of _____, 193___

Signature _____

_____
(Name, grade, and organization, typed or stamped) Company Commander.

Company _____ Camp _____ Date _____

I accept reenrollment in the Civilian Conservation Corps for the period ending at the discretion of the United States between _____ under the same conditions as my previous enrollment.

_____
(Enrollee's signature)

Reenrolled this _____ day of _____, 193___

Signature _____

_____
(Name, grade, and organization, typed or stamped) Company Commander.

IV. RECORD OF SERVICE

From 7-8-39 to 10-3-39 under War Department 570 Company at Camp Bitely F-22 (Mich)
Type of work Reforestation Manner of performance Satisfactory
Transferred to 610th Co CCC SCS-7 Ill per paragraph 1 S. O. 77 Left Company 570
October 3, 1939 Last paid to include 9-30-39 on voucher No. 73 Oct , 1939
accounts of CAPT J. W. McManus FA-R. Due U. S. for clothing and equipment, $ None for AWOL on
$ _____ ; for AWOP on _____, $ _____ ; per E H dated _____, $ _____ ; due CCC store _____
Company, $ _____ Due company fund _____ Company, $ _____ ; other indebtedness, $ _____ I have verified the foregoing entries.
(Signature) (Name typed) (Grade and organization)
Remarks None

Foregoing indebtedness entered on {P/R / F/S} _____ (Date) _____ (Initials)

4. Record of Service

XIII. DISCHARGE

Enrollee is a satisfactory worker.

_____ XXXX __L. Buckley__ __Proj. Superintendent__
(Signature) (Name typed) (Grade and organization)

ENROLLEE'S TRANSPORTATION STATEMENT

I elect "To be furnished transportation to __CHICAGO, ILL__ and I agree to accept the transportation elected and furnished as full and complete settlement of the Government's obligation to furnish me transportation.

~~"Not to be furnished transportation, and I hereby waive any right to transportation in~~

_____
Harold L. Washington CC6-269318

CERTIFICATE OF EMPLOYMENT

COMPANY COMMANDER'S CERTIFICATE (for use when appropriate):

I certify that I have investigated the (offer of employment) (urgent and proper call) (intention to return to school)" of this enrollee and that I am satisfied that it is bona fide.

Signature _____

_____
(Name, grade, and organization, typed or stamped) Company Commander.

Remarks: __Orientation talk given: July 3, 1939__
__F. B. I. taken: July 10, 1939__
__Previous enrollments: None__
__Occupational qualifications: Laborer__
__Provisions of Par. 40 d WD CCC Regulations 1937 read to enrollee and CCC Form 15__
__signed and filed with Individual Records July 4, 1939__

TYPE OF DISCHARGE: °Honorable; ~~administrative~~; ~~dishonorable~~.   610th Company, C.C.C.
Camp Stockton, SCS-7 (Ill)

DISCHARGED __DEC 22 1939__ (date) from __610th__ Company, C. C. C. Camp __Stockton, Illinois__

__Sparta CCC__ District, because of __EXPIRATION OF TERM OF ENROLLMENT FOR CONVENIENCE OF U.S.__

Transportation furnished from __Stockton, Illinois__ to __CHICAGO, ILL__

Final statement (final payment roll)" to include __DEC 22 1939__, 193_, forwarded to the Finance Officer,

at __Sparta, Wisconsin__ on __DEC 22 1939__ 193_

Enrollee has been notified that he cannot be again accepted for enrollment for a period of 1-year. ____
(Initials)

Signature __T. A. RATHJE__
C. C. C. Company Commander

_____
(Name, grade, and organization, typed or stamped) Company Commander.

XIV. SIGNATURE OF OFFICERS INITIALING ENTRIES

Initials	Signature	Name typed or printed
		P. L. Johnson, 2 Lt. Inf-Res.
		T. A. RATHJE
		C. C. C. Company

° Line out the uses inapplicable.

5. Discharge Records

From OCT 1939 to DEC 22 1939 under WAR Department 612th Company at Camp Stockton, Stockton, Ill.
Type of work Soil Erosion (Laborer) Manner of performance SATISFACTORY
Transferred to DISCHARGED per paragraph 1 S. O. Left Company 4
DEC 22 1939 Last paid to include DEC 22 1939 on voucher No. P-E/R December, 1939.
accounts of D.H. Parsall, Capt. Fin-Res. Due U. S. for clothing and equipment, $ _____; for AWOL on _____
$ NOTHING for AWOP on _____, $ NOTHING per R/H dated _____, $ NOTHING due CCC store 612th
Company, $ NOTHING Due company fund 612th Company, $ NOTHING other indebtedness, $ NOTHING I have verified the foregoing entries.

T. A. RATHJE
C. C. C.

Remarks NOTHING
Foregoing indebtedness entered on {P/R} FINAL DEC 22 1939

APPENDIX C

MILITARY SERVICE RECORD OF HAROLD WASHINGTON
15 Feb 1943 - 20 Jan 1946

1. Sailing Time Table Map in the Pacific and Far East

2. Separation Qualification Record
    — Summary of Military Occupation
    — Military Education
    — Civilian Education
    — Civilian Occupations

3. Enlisted Record and Report of Separation Honorable Discharge
    — Military History
    — Decorations and Citations
    — Mustering Out Pay

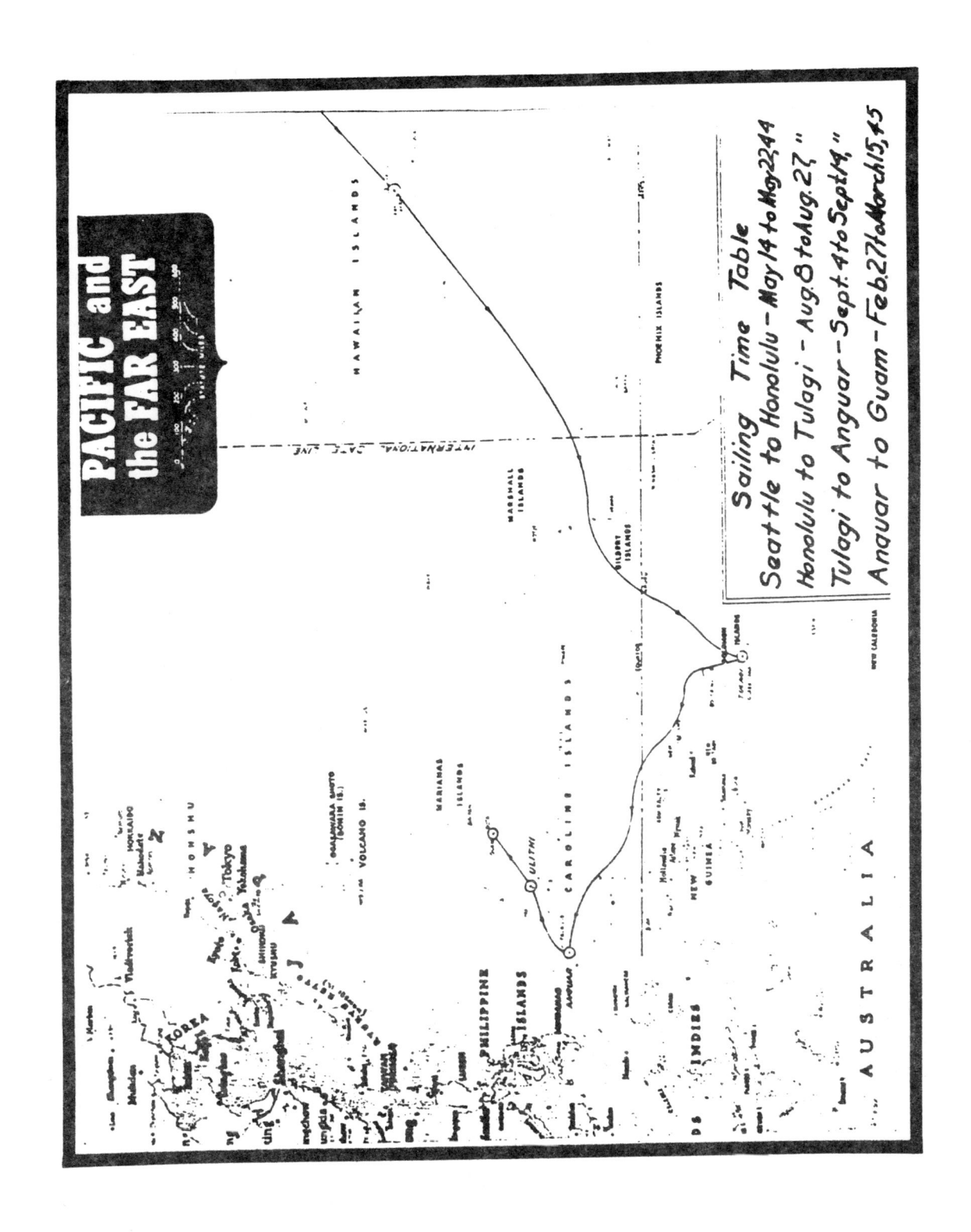

1. Sailing Time Table Map in the Pacific and Far East

Army of the United States

SEPARATION QUALIFICATION RECORD
SAVE THIS FORM. IT WILL NOT BE REPLACED IF LOST

This record of job assignments and special training received in the Army is furnished to the soldier when he leaves the service. In its preparation, information is taken from available Army records and supplemented by personal interview. The information about civilian education and work experience is based on the individual's own statements. The veteran may present this document to former employers, prospective employers, representatives of schools or colleges, or use it in any other way that may prove beneficial to him.

1. LAST NAME—FIRST NAME—MIDDLE INITIAL			MILITARY OCCUPATIONAL ASSIGNMENTS		
WASHINGTON HAROLD			10. MONTHS	11. GRADE	12. MILITARY OCCUPATIONAL SPECIALTY
2. ARMY SERIAL NO.	3. GRADE	4. SOCIAL SECURITY No.	3	PVT	Basic 521
36 795 331	1 SGT	352 05 4930	8	Cpl	Technician Camouflage 804
5. PERMANENT MAILING ADDRESS (Street, City, County, State)			2	SGT	Chemical N C O 870
111 East 44th St Chicago 15 Ill			17	T 3	Physics Laboratory 1601
6. DATE OF ENTRY INTO ACTIVE SERVICE	7. DATE OF SEPARATION	8. DATE OF BIRTH	5	1 SGT	First Sgt 502
15 Feb 43	20 Jan 46	15 Apr 22			
9. PLACE OF SEPARATION					
Camp Grant Ill					

SUMMARY OF MILITARY OCCUPATIONS

13. TITLE—DESCRIPTION—RELATED CIVILIAN OCCUPATION

PHYSICS LABORATORY TECHNICIAN 160
  Supervised in physical testing and experimental work in a military equipment for tests on soil to determine the specific gravity, plastic and liquid limits, California bearing ratio, sive-analysis tests, density tests, concrete analysis tests.
ADMINISTRATIVE N C O   502
  Supervised the administrative work to be done in a company orderly room.

WD AGO FORM 100   This form supersedes WD AGO Form 100, 15 July 1944, which will not be used.

2. Separation Qualification Record

MILITARY EDUCATION

14. NAME OR TYPE OF SCHOOL—COURSE OR CURRICULUM—DURATION—DESCRIPTION

Attended a camauflage School at March Field California for 2 weeks
Also attended a Sails Mechanic School, for 5 weeks at March Field.

CIVILIAN EDUCATION

15. HIGHEST GRADE COMPLETED	16. DEGREES OR DIPLOMAS	17. YEAR LEFT SCHOOL
12	Diploma	1942

18. NAME AND ADDRESS OF LAST SCHOOL ATTENDED
Du Sable H S Chicago Ill

19. MAJOR COURSES OF STUDY
Academic

OTHER TRAINING OR SCHOOLING

20. COURSE—NAME AND ADDRESS OF SCHOOL—DATE	21. DURATION

CIVILIAN OCCUPATIONS

22. TITLE—NAME AND ADDRESS OF EMPLOYER—INCLUSIVE DATES—DESCRIPTION

FILE CLERK
    Employed by the Government (civil service) as a file clerk to work in the United States Treasury Department, Merchandise Mart. Bldg, Chicago Ill. Handled a special machine for use in stamping Government War Bonds, as to address of owner, number of Bond and other Data.

RECEIVED VETERANS ADMINISTRATION
VOC. REHAB.
CHICAGO, ILLINOIS
MAR 5 1946

ADDITIONAL INFORMATION

23. REMARKS

24. SIGNATURE OF PERSON BEING SEPARATED
Harold Washington

25. SIGNATURE OF SEPARATION CLASSIFICATION OFFICER

26. NAME OF OFFICER (Typed or Stamped)
CLYDE W MILLS CPT AC

ENLISTED RECORD AND REPORT OF SEPARATION
HONORABLE DISCHARGE

1. LAST NAME - FIRST NAME - MIDDLE INITIAL	2. ARMY SERIAL NO.	3. GRADE	4. ARM OR SERVICE	5. COMPONENT
WASHINGTON HAROLD	36 795 331	SGT	CE	AUS

6. ORGANIZATION	7. DATE OF SEPARATION	8. PLACE OF SEPARATION
CO C 1887TH ENGR AVN BN	20 JAN 46	SEPARATION CENTER CAMP GRANT ILLINOIS

9. PERMANENT ADDRESS FOR MAILING PURPOSES	10. DATE OF BIRTH	11. PLACE OF BIRTH
111 EAST 44TH ST CHICAGO 15 ILL	15 APR 22	CHICAGO ILL

12. ADDRESS FROM WHICH EMPLOYMENT WILL BE SOUGHT	13. COLOR EYES	14. COLOR HAIR	15. HEIGHT	16. WEIGHT	17. NO. DEPEND.
SEE 9	BROWN	BLACK	5 9	165	

18. RACE	19. MARITAL STATUS	20. U.S. CITIZEN	21. CIVILIAN OCCUPATION AND NO.
NEGRO (X)	MARRIED (X)	YES	FILE CLERK 1 17.01

MILITARY HISTORY

22. DATE OF INDUCTION	23. DATE OF ENLISTMENT	24. DATE OF ENTRY INTO ACTIVE SERVICE	25. PLACE OF ENTRY INTO SERVICE
8 FEB 43		15 FEB 43	FT CUSTER MICH

26. REGISTERED	27. LOCAL S.S. BOARD NO.	28. COUNTY AND STATE	29. HOME ADDRESS AT TIME OF ENTRY INTO SERVICE
YES	84	COOK CO ILL	SEE 9

30. MILITARY OCCUPATIONAL SPECIALTY	31. MILITARY QUALIFICATION AND DATE
ADMIN NCO 502 PHYSICS LABORATORY TECH 160	M W/RIFLE M 1

32. BATTLES AND CAMPAIGNS
STERN MANDATES

33. DECORATIONS AND CITATIONS
3 OVERSEAS SERVICE BARS AMERICAN CAMPAIGN MEDAL ASIATIC PACIFIC THEATER RIBBON GOOD CONDUCT MEDAL WORLD WAR II VICTORY MEDAL

34. WOUNDS RECEIVED IN ACTION
NONE

35. LATEST IMMUNIZATION DATES
SMALLPOX	TYPHOID	TETANUS	OTHER
DEC 44	OCT 45	DEC 44	

36. SERVICE OUTSIDE CONTINENTAL U.S. AND RETURN
DATE OF DEPARTURE	DESTINATION	DATE OF ARRIVAL
13 MAY 44		22 MAY 44
1 JAN 46		14 JAN 46

37. TOTAL LENGTH OF SERVICE
CONTINENTAL SERVICE	FOREIGN SERVICE
YEARS 1 MONTHS 3 DAYS 4	YEARS 1 MONTHS 8 DAYS 2

38. HIGHEST GRADE HELD
1ST SGT

39. PRIOR SERVICE
NONE

40. REASON AND AUTHORITY FOR SEPARATION
CONV OF GOVT RR 1-1 (DEMOBILIZATION) AR 615-365 DTD 15 DEC 44

41. SERVICE SCHOOLS ATTENDED
CAMOUFLAGE 2 WKS 43   SOILS MECHANIC 5 WKS 43

42. EDUCATION (Years)
Grammar 8 High School 4 College 0

PAY DATA   VOU #21056

43. LONGEVITY FOR PAY PURPOSES	44. MUSTERING OUT PAY	45. SOLDIERS DEPOSITS	46. TRAVEL PAY	47. TOTAL AMOUNT, NAME OF DISBURSING OFFICER
YEARS 2 MONTHS 11 DAYS 13	TOTAL 300 THIS PAYMENT 100	NONE	$4.40	$183.88 G F DOLBEAR CAPT FD

INSURANCE NOTICE
IMPORTANT: IF PREMIUM IS NOT PAID WHEN DUE OR WITHIN THIRTY-ONE DAYS THEREAFTER, INSURANCE WILL LAPSE. MAKE CHECKS OR MONEY ORDERS PAYABLE TO THE TREASURER OF THE U.S. AND FORWARD TO COLLECTIONS SUBDIVISION, VETERANS ADMINISTRATION, WASHINGTON 25, D.C.

48. KIND OF INSURANCE	49. HOW PAID	50. Effective Date of Allotment Discontinuance	51. Date of Next Premium Due (One month after 50)	52. PREMIUM DUE EACH MONTH	53. INTENTION OF VETERAN TO
Nat. Serv. X U.S. Govt. None	Allotment X Direct to V.A.	31 JAN 46	28 FEB 46	6.70	Continue X

55. REMARKS
LAPEL BUTTON ISSUED   ASR SCORE (2 SEP 45) 52
INACTIVE STATUS ERC FROM 8 FEB 43 TO 14 FEB 43

56. SIGNATURE OF PERSON BEING SEPARATED

57. PERSONNEL OFFICER
AMELIA ANTHONY 1ST LT WAC

WD AGO FORM 53-55
1 November 1944

5. VETERANS ADMINISTRATION REGIONAL OFFICE COPY

3. Enlisted Record and Report of Separation Honorable Discharge

APPENDIX D

HAROLD WASHINGTON'S ANCESTRY

PLACE SORTED LIST

Harold Washington's Ancestry Place Sorted List

Place	Event	Date	Name
AR	Birth	Apr 1877	HAMILTON, Lula
AR/MS	Birth	Apr 1878	WEEKS, Arbella D.
IL	Death	After 1910	, Carolin
	Birth	About 1899	HAMILTON, Daniel
	Birth	About 1868	HAMILTON, Jesse
	Birth	About 1900	HAMILTON, McGowan
	Death	After 1910	HAMILTON, Samuel
	Death	About 1875	HAMILTON, Warren
	Marriage	About 1910	SUIT, Jessie & WASHINGTON, Artimis
	Birth	About 1904	WHEELER, Ethel
	Birth	About 1906	WHEELER, Prentess
IL, Cook, Chicago	Death	10 Sep 1980	JONES, Bertha
	Birth	19 Oct 1920	WASHINGTON, Edward Glyn
	Death	6 Mar 1947	WASHINGTON, Edward Glyn
	Marriage	22 Jul 1942	WASHINGTON, Harold Lee & FINCH, Nancy Dorothy
	Birth	15 Apr 1922	WASHINGTON, Harold Lee
	Death	25 Nov 1987	WASHINGTON, Harold Lee
	Death	7 Nov 1953	WASHINGTON, Roy L.
	Marriage	1 Jul 1933	WASHINGTON, Roy L. & JACKSON, Arlene
IL, Cook, Chicago, Lincoln Cemetery	Burial	8 Mar 1947	WASHINGTON, Edward Glyn
	Burial		WASHINGTON, Roy L.
IL, Cook, Dolton, Oakland Cemetery	Burial	15 Sep 1980	JONES, Bertha
IL, Jackson, Murphysboro	Birth	27 Feb 1898	JONES, Bertha

Place	Event	Date	Name
IL,	Birth	Apr 1881	HAMILTON, Boyd
Massac,	Birth	Apr 1889/91	HAMILTON, Bryant
Brooklyn	Birth	Feb 1879	HAMILTON, Lida
	Birth	Apr 1887	HAMILTON, Uren
	Birth	Jan 1883	HAMILTON, Wade
IL,	Death	About 1913	HOWELL, Mary Jane Elizabeth
Massac,	Birth	20 Sep 1904	WASHINGTON, Booker T.
Brook-	Birth	About 1903	WASHINGTON, Georgia
port	Death	27 Jun 1903	WASHINGTON, Isam/Isham
	Burial	28 Jun 1903	WASHINGTON, Isam/Isham
	Birth	Mar 1894	WASHINGTON, William
IL,	Marriage	29 Jul 1916	WASHINGTON, Roy L. & JONES, Bertha
Saline,	Birth	1916	WASHINGTON, Roy L., Junior
Carrier Mills			
IL, Sangamon, Springfield	Death	1 Jul 1952	WEEKS, Arbella D.
IL, Sangamon, Springfield, Oak Ridge Cemetery	Burial	5 Jul 1952	WEEKS, Arbella D.
IL?	Marriage	About 1865	HAMILTON, Samuel & , Carolin
	Marriage	About 1879	HAMILTON, Sep & ROBINSON, Elizabeth
	Marriage	Before 1898	JONES, Rederick & BARKER, Adeline
KY	Marriage	About 1870	FRASIER, Woodson & HOWELL, Mary Jane Elizabeth
	Birth	About 1848	HALL, Cata
	Birth	About 1868	HAMILTON, Joseph
	Birth	About 1824	HAMILTON, Samuel
	Birth	Mar 1848	HAMILTON, Sep
	Birth	May 1850	HOWELL, Mary Jane Elizabeth
	Birth	Aug 1887	STAHL, Florence
	Birth	1860	STAHL, John
	Birth	Jul 1883	STAHL, Marthe S.
	Birth	Mar 1896	WASHINGTON, "Exey"
	Birth	May 1887	WASHINGTON, Artimis
	Birth	About 1863	WASHINGTON, Ed
	Birth	1855/1860	WASHINGTON, Eliza
	Birth	Jan 1889	WASHINGTON, Eva

Place	Event	Date	Name
	Birth	Oct 1893	WASHINGTON, Ezekiel
	Marriage	About 1860	WASHINGTON, I. & NEAL, Rebecca
	Birth	About 1873	WASHINGTON, Ida
	Birth	About 1865	WASHINGTON, J. Albert
	Birth		WASHINGTON, John Ray
KY, Ballard	Marriage	27 Feb 1893	BLANK, Henry & WASHINGTON, Ida
	Marriage	25 Dec 1903	EASLEY, Thomas & WASHINGTON, Avella
	Death	Aug 1885	FRASIER, Woodson
	Marriage	26 Dec 1876	HALL, Cata & WASHINGTON, Eliza
	Death	24 Nov 1885	NEAL, Rebecca
	Marriage	8 Mar 1886	STAHL, John & WASHINGTON, Sallie
	Marriage	About 1885	WASHINGTON, I. & HOWELL, Mary Jane Elizabeth
	Birth	2 May 1875	WASHINGTON, Isom McDaniel
	Marriage	6 Jun 1885	WASHINGTON, J.A. & STAHL, Ida
	Birth	Dec 1888	WASHINGTON, Schooler G.
	Marriage	About 1886	WASHINGTON, William and ___, Georgia
KY, Ballard, Hinkleville	Birth	2 Aug 1871	WASHINGTON, Mary Jane
	Birth	Jan 1870	WASHINGTON, Sallie
	Birth	12 Jan 1867	WASHINGTON, William Pleasant
KY, Ballard, Lovelaceville	Birth	Oct 1899	WASHINGTON, Elizabeth "Lizzie"
	Birth	17 Feb 1873	WASHINGTON, Horace Lee
	Birth	12 Apr 1897	WASHINGTON, Roy L.
MI, Macomb, Lincoln Memorial	Burial	2 Mar 1954	WASHINGTON, Elizabeth "Lizzie"
MI, Wayne, Detroit	Death	25 Feb 1954	WASHINGTON, Elizabeth "Lizzie"
MO, St.Louis, St.Louis	Death	14 Jul 1962	WASHINGTON, Booker T.
	Death	28 Apr 1957	WASHINGTON, Isom McDaniel
MO, St.Louis, St.Louis, Greenwood Cemetery	Burial	2 May 1957	WASHINGTON, Isom McDaniel

Place	Event	Date	Name
MO, St.Louis, Washington Park	Burial		WASHINGTON, Booker T.
NC	Birth	About 1828	,Carolin
	Birth	About 1800	,Mary Rose
	Birth	Jun 1832	WASHINGTON, Isam/Isham
TN	Birth	About 1874	SUIT, Jessie
TN or KY	Birth	About 1847-1851	ROBINSON, Elizabeth Lizzie

GLOSSARY

African Methodist Episcopal (A.M.E.): a church denomination organized by Richard Allen in 1794 and primarily made up of African-Americans.

African-American: pertains to Americans whose ancestors descended from the continent of Africa.

Ancestor: pertains to one of a person's direct family line who has lived before him (parents, grandparents, etc.).

Archives: a place where a collection of records is stored.

Autobiography: the life story of a person written by that person.

Biography: a written history of a person's life written by someone else.

Census: an official count of all the people living in a designated area at a specific time. The first federal census in the U.S. was in 1790, which listed the heads of a household only, and (in 1850) the number of other persons in the household. The first Census count for Blacks (ex-slaves) as heads of their households in the United States was 1870. (The 1890 Census was destroyed by fire.)

City Directory: a published list of all the residents of a city, usually published annually, giving the name, address, occupation, and sometimes race of each citizen.

Civil War: a war between the Northern and Southern states of the United States, 1861-1865.

Divorce: a legal process by which a marriage contract between a man and a woman is dissolved (separated) by law.

Family tradition: a belief or legend passed down by word of mouth from generation to generation in a family.

Genealogy: the study of origins and descent of families.

Maiden name: the last name of a woman before marriage; her father's last name.

Maternal: pertains to the mother's side of the family.

Memorabilia: items of personal family value such as old photographs, old letters, and other items.

Migration: the movement from one location to another within the same country. Many African-Americans migrated to the northern states after the Civil War.

Negro: pertaining to members of the Black race whose ancestors were from Africa.

Obituary: a published announcement, usually appearing in a newspaper, of a person's death, with a brief account of his or her life.

Oral history: a collection of information about the past events through oral sources such as oral and written interviews.

Paternal: on the father's side of the family.

Pedigree chart: a form designed to record one's direct ancestors and genealogical information such as names as well as birth, death and marriage dates and locations.

Primary record: a record made at the time of the event, such as birth, marriage, and death.

Secondary record: a record, such as a book or newspaper article, written after the event by someone who was not present when the event occurred.

Soundex: an index that groups together surnames that sound alike but are spelled differently. There is a separate Soundex for each state. Within each state surnames are grouped alphabetically by the first letter. Under that letter surnames of the same or similar sounds but of variant spellings are grouped by numerical code. Within each numerical code individuals are arranged alphabetically by given name and, within given names, alphabetically by state of birth. By using the Soundex code one may be able to locate his or her ancestors in most states, regardless of spelling. (A complete description of the Soundex system is included in the microfilm catalogs published by the National Archives.)

Surname: a person's last name inherited at birth; usually the father passes on his surname to his children.

BIBLIOGRAPHY

Blockson, Charles and Ron Fry. *Black genealogy*. Englewood Cliffs, NJ: Prentice-Hall, Inc., 1977.

Cerny, Johni. "From Maria to Bill Cosby: A case study in tracing Black slave ancestry," *The National Genealogical Society Quarterly*, Vol. 75, No. 1 (March 1987). Arlington, VA: National Genealogical Society.

Cerny, Johni. "Black American research." In *The source: A guidebook of American genealogy*, edited by Arlene Eakle and Johni Cerny. Salt Lake City, UT: Ancestry Publishing, 1985.

Doane, Gilbert H. and James B. Bell. *Searching for your ancestors: The how and why of genealogy*. Minneapolis, Minn.: University of Minnesota Press, 1988.

Douglass, Frederick. *My bondage and my freedom*. Urbana and Chicago, IL: University of Illinois Press, 1987.

Everton, George B., Sr. *The handy book for genealogists*. Logan, UT: Everton, 1981.

Greenwood, Val D. *The researcher's guide to American genealogy*. Baltimore, MD: Genealogical Publishing Co., 1973.

Gutman, Herbert G. *The Black family in slavery and freedom*. New York: Vintage Books, 1976.

Haley, Alex. *Roots*. Garden City, NY: Doubleday, 1976.

Howard, Victor B. *Black liberation in Kentucky: Emancipation and freedom, 1862-1884*. Lexington, KY: University of Kentucky Press, 1983.

Magee, Juliette M. *Ballard's brave boys*. Wickliffe, KY: The Advance-Yeoman: Kentucky Historical Society (Ref. 976 90213 189M). Frankfort, KY, 1974.

Mills, Elizabeth Shown and Gary B. Mills. "The genealogical assessment of Alex Haley's Roots," *National Genealogical Society Quarterly*, Vol. 72, No. 1 (March 1984). Arlington, VA: National Genealogical Society.

Rose, James and Alice Eicholz. *Black Genesis*. Detroit, MI: Gale Research Co., 1978.

Speed, Thomas. *Union regiments of Kentucky*. Louisville, KY: Courier Journal: Kentucky Historical Society (Ref. 976 901 U 58Y). Frankfort, KY, 1897.

Streets, David H. *Slave genealogy: A research guide with case studies*. Bowie, MD: Heritage, 1986.

Tippie, Gwendolyn. *Afro-American births, Adair thru Ballard County, Kentucky, 1852-1862*. Salt Lake City, UT: IDS Church Genealogical Dept., 1980.

Travis, Dempsey J. *Harold, the people's mayor: The authorized biography of Mayor Harold Washington*. Chicago: Urban Research Press, Inc., 1989.

Walls, William J. *The African Methodist Episcopal Zion Church: The reality of the Black church*. Charlotte, NC: A.M.E. Zion Publishing House, 1974.

Walker, James D. *Black genealogy: How to begin*. Athens, GA: Independent Study, University of Georgia Center for Continuing Education, 1977.

INDEX

----, Carolin 103 106 Georgia 105 Mary Rose 106
ALLEN, Richard 107
ANDERSON, Benj 17 Doc 17 Elihu 17 Troy 17 Wm 17
BARKER, Adeline 43 104
BILLINGTON, B F 65 B Frank 63
BLANK, Henry 52 105 Ida 52 105
BROWN, Charles V 34
CASEY, Samuel 17
CHEEFUS, John P 30
CLINGHAM, Mr 17 Mrs 17
CURRY, Carl R 17
CURTIS, Mr 17 Mrs 17
DALEY, Richard J 39
DUSABLE, Jean Point 30
EASLEY, Avella 52 105 Thomas 52 105
EMMETT, Marie 22
FINCH, Nancy Dorothy 28 31 32 40 43 103
FLINT, Ben 65
FRASER, Fannie 58 Fany 58 Woodson 56 58
FRASIER, 60 Dock 62 Elizabeth 52 56 Mary Elizabeth 52 67 Mary Jane Elizabeth 9 13 68 Woodson 9 13 72 104 105
GIBSON, Tom 58
GOINS, Clifton 17
GREGG, J A 26
HACKLEY, R H 19
HALL, Cata 104 105 Eliza 105
HAMILTON, Albert 78 Arbella 16 42 48 76 78 79 80 81 Boid 78 80 Boyd 79 81 104 Bryant 78 80 104 Carolin 78 79 80 104 Daniel 79 103 Elizabeth 79 80 104 Elizabeth Lizzie 43 Elizzie 78 79 Ibeller 78

HAMILTON (Continued)
Jesse 78 79 103 Joseph 16 78 79 80 104 Lida 76 78 79 80 104 Lidey 80 Lidey E 78 Lizzie 76 78 79 81 Louley 78 Lula 78 80 103 Lydia 81 Marry Ros 78 Mary R 78 Mary Rose 80 McGowan 79 103 Nelley J 78 Samuel 78 79 80 103 104 Sep 16 42 43 76 78 79 80 81 104 Sip 79 Uren 78 80 104 Wade 78 80 104 Warren 79 103 Warren H 78
HARRIS, Lewis 17
HOPKINS, John 62
HOWARD, Armade 73
HOWELL, Elizabeth 72 Mary Elizabeth 52 67 Mary Jane Elizabeth 9 13 68 104 105
HUSBAND, W Y 65
HUTCHERSON, A G 63
JACKSON, Arlene 21 26 27 28 103
JETT, Albert 10
JOHNSON, Elizabeth 20 21 27 Lizzie 24 28 Nelson 21
JONES, Adeline 43 104 Bertha 21 22 23 27 28 43 48 103 104 Rederick 43 104
KIMMEL, John 61
KING, Martin Luther Jr 39
LEE, D T 57
LINCOLN, 74
LOVELACE, George 62 Hanon 63 V A 10 Widow 61 62
MATTHEW, 73
MORGAN, J H 60
MORRIS, Evelyn 17 James 17 Martha 17
NEAL, Rebecca 8 11 14 43 60 68 105

NEELY, F J 65
PETERS, 60
PETREE, J S 7 60 John S 7 60
PORTEE, Blanch 17 Harl 17 Robert 17
PRESTON, J S 64 John 61 62 John S 65
REEVES, 65 Robert 58 61 62
RICH, Widow 63
ROBINSON, Elizabeth 16 79 80 81 104 Elizabeth Lizzie 43 106
RUSS, Jno 63
SENOR, Mrs 20 Roberta 19
SMITH, Bugg 61 John 61
STAHL, Florence 72 104 Ida 52 105 John 12 52 72 73 104 105 Martha S 72 Marthe S 104 Sallie 12 21 52 56 59 72 73 105
SUIT, Artimis 103 Jessie 103 106
SWAFFORD, John 65
SYDES, J H 19
TANN, Joseph 17
TAYLOR, Maud 79
THOMPKINS, Wm 17
TREWALLA, 61 62 63 64 Bros 12
VANLOOY, E H 13
WALLS, Jeff 17
WASHINGTON, Albert 52 53 58 64 Arbella 11 13 14 16 17 19 20 21 22 48 53 74 76 77 81 Arbella D 43 Arbella H 50 Ardie 73 Arlene 21 26 27 28 103 Artimis 11 16 51 103 104 Avella 52 105 Bertha 21 22 23 24 27 28 43 48 52 104 Booker 19 81 Booker T 16 20 21 22 27 53 68 73 74 79 104 105 106 Dan 56 Daniel 56 Ed 12 104 Edward 24 27 Edward Glen 28 Edward Glyn 103 Eliza 104 105 Elizabeth 9 11 14 16 19 20 21 22 27 52 56 60 72 73 Elizabeth Lizzie 105 Eva 73 104 Exey 73 104 Ezekiel 11 16 105 Ezekiel R 51 Frank 56 Geneva 20 24 27 28 George 76 Georgia 73 104 105 Harold 20 24 30 31 32 33 34 35 36 37 39 40 41 47 48 54 76 85 95 101 Harold L 29

WASHINGTON (Continued)
Harold Lee 28 40 42 43 87 103 Horace 72 79 80 81 Horace L 12 Horace Lee 8 13 105 Horrance Lee 68 I 56 105 I A D 48 I M D 19 20 21 22 I Mack D 19 56 I W P 65 Ida 12 52 105 Isaac 48 Isam 7 8 9 10 11 13 14 16 22 43 48 50 51 53 54 55 56 57 58 59 60 61 63 67 69 71 74 76 Isam Mack 68 Isam Mack D 12 53 72 Isam McDaniel 8 Isam McDaniel (Mack D) 14 21 Isam/Isham 64 68 72 104 106 Isham 7 11 12 43 56 57 58 59 60 61 62 63 66 73 81 Isham/Isam 81 Ism 63 Isom 7 11 12 52 Isom D 73 Isom M D 73 74 Isom Mack D 12 50 53 Isom McDaniel 13 43 68 81 105 Isom McDaniel (Mack D) 14 J A 64 105 J Albert 12 59 105 Jef 56 John Ray 8 11 12 59 62 105 Lizzie 16 21 24 50 53 Mack 11 14 16 17 19 20 22 27 48 50 51 53 56 76 77 78 81 Mack D 51 52 73 Marie 19 22 Mary 12 Mary Elizabeth 52 67 70 Mary J 50 51 52 Mary Jane 8 13 68 105 Mary Jane Elizabeth 9 13 105 Nancy 36 Nancy Dorothy 28 31 32 40 43 103 Nettie 73 Pvt 32 Rebecca 8 9 11 14 43 60 68 105 Rev 19 Reverend 17 Roy 22 23 24 25 26 27 28 40 48 50 53 Roy Jr 24 27 104 Roy L 16 20 21 27 28 32 43 48 49 52 53 54 103 104 105 Roy L Jr 27 Sallie 8 12 52 68 72 105 Sally 21 Salvany 12 68 Schooler 11 14 16 50 Schooler G 9 13 51 72 105 W P 65 William 12 16 65 73 104 105 William P 59 73 74 William Pleasant 8 12 68 105
WATSON, Bertha Maria 20 Francine Louise 20 Francis 27 Geneva 20 27 Richard Allen 20 Travis Lercy 20 Wm Arnold 20

112

WEEKS, Arbella 13 14 21 22 77 79 80 Arbella D 42 43 79 81 103 104 Elizabeth 16 79 80 81 Louley 80 Lula 16 Smith 14 76 78 79 80 81

WHEELER, Ethel 80 81 103 Lydia 79 81 Prentess 80 103 Prentice 81
WIMBERLEY, Joseph 17

F
548.54
.W36
B73
1993
Copy 2